Tuxedo Junction

Tuxedo Junction

The Lords of Antartica

Gloria Clifford

To order additional copies of this book, contact:
Xlibris Corporation
1-888-795-4274
www.Xlibris.com
Orders@Xlibris.com
54300

CONTENTS

Dedication

I wish to dedicate this book and film to my deceased husband, Richard Clifford, who was a wonderful travel companion. Of all our expedition cruises we both agreed that the cruise we took in 1992 from Ushuaia, Argentina to the Falkland Islands and down the Peninsula to Faraday Station was our favorite. That is when we fell in love with penguins.

ACKNOWLEDGEMENT

Special thanks to my mentor, Tony Soper, an Ornithologist. He was on the Expedition staff and wrote the log of this adventure. Tony is an outstanding Naturalist in England. He created, wrote and directed the BBS Nature series. He allowed me to use information from his log for this book. I am very grateful.

Thanks also to Rod Ledingham, Field Operations, who took me by the hand and advised me what I needed to do to take great pictures. I needed his advice.

Also, thanks to Susan Adie, our Expedition Leader and Quark Expeditions.

PREFACE

My love for adventure I now know must come from my inherited genes. In Antarctica there are five places named after my family names. First, my maiden name is Neff, which is Swiss, and there is a Neff's Canyon in Lake County. Secondly, there is Douglas Range and Douglas Peninsula and I belong to the Douglas Clan. There is a third gene from my mother's maiden name of Evans and there is a Cape Evans on Ross Island and an Evans Peninsula. Also I was born in Ohio and there is an Ohio Range.

It was destiny that I would go to and love Antarctica. The first time I went to Antarctica only 6, 000 tourists had cruised there and in 2003 there were 13, 571 and this past year 20, 000. I have been to Antarctica two times. Only 5% of all these passengers have been to the Ross Sea area. I cruised on the Kapitan Khlebnikov, a Russian Icebreaker, through the Ross Sea for five days to reach Cape Washington, Coulman Island and B-15A Iceberg. There are two Russian Icebreakers and they can go through this sea of ice.

People have always questioned me as to why I would go to Antarctica when I live in sunny Southern California on the ocean. They all say it is so cold. I was skier, tried cross country (too tiring) and because I love the snow and mountains I ended up snowmobiling in the Grand Tetons. Again I went into areas where the only way you go there was by snowmobile in the winter and horseback riding in the summer. This was along the continental divide.

I have all the thermals, wool sweaters, and boots to keep me warm. They gave me a parka on board the ship so the only exposure was small areas on my face. Pictures show me with very little exposure to the wind . . . I even had hand warmers in my gloves. Needless to say I was prepared.

I truly like to get away from our busy civilization. I know of no place that is such a contrast to our life in the world today. Antarctica is the most beautiful place on earth. The quiet is so peaceful—no city noises. I became part of that nature scene.

I am a world traveler and have seen over 130 countries. I have been to most of the famous art museums, historical sites and antiquities of the past. I have such love of life that I want to experience all this earth has to offer.

Antarctica and the penguins are to me the most serene place on earth . . . .

CERTIFICATE OF ACHIEVEMENT

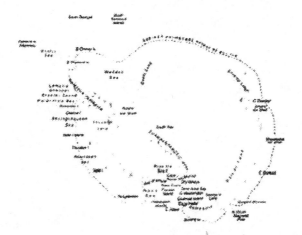

Awarded to

Gloria L Clifford

while traveling on board the I/B *Kapitan Khlebnikov* for

Crossing the Antarctic Circle at
66°33' S & 173°57' E on 10/12/03
Landing on the Antarctic Continent at Cape Adare
71°18' S & 170°10' E on 11/12/03

Furthest South at Iceberg B-15A
75° 57' S & 168° 50' E on 15/12/03

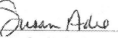

Expedition Leader

Captain

Why would a 76-year-old woman go by herself and endure the weather, the roughest seas in the world to see and film the Emperor penguins? This is my story of that adventure

CHAPTER 1

This trip was a total of flying 14,931 miles round trip from Los Angeles, California to Hobart, Tasmania and return from Auckland, New Zealand to Los Angeles. My sea journey was 5,365 nautical miles. There were 5 days of sailing through a sea of ice and the rest was sailing through the roughest seas in the world. We sailed from Hobart to the Ross Sea. Our furthest point south was the largest iceberg in the world called B15A. I will write about this later as it has become newsworthy.

I have traveled to over 130 countries and many of these trips have been expedition cruises to many places like the Arctic, Greenland, Alaska, and in New Zealand to Milford Sound, Doubtful Sound. I have crossed the Tasmania Sea to Australia all the way up the Barrier Reef Islands to Cairns. I snorkeled and hiked through those islands.

I have cruised and snorkeled through the South Sea Islands of Tahiti, Moorea, and Bora Bora. In addition, I snorkeled in the Caribbean, Costa Rica and the Bahamas. I do like warm water and those beautiful tropical fish.

My husband and I cruised in 1992 from Ushuaia to the Falkland Islands, South Georgia, South Shetland Island, Livingston Island, also to Deception Island, Paula Island down the Neumayer and Lemaire Channel to Peterman Island in Antarctica. We went as far south as Paradise Bay. There we went ashore to what was then the British Research Station called Faraday. This is where they discovered the ozone hole. At this station, I actually saw where they lay on their backs under a hole in the ceiling and measured the ozone hole. I wonder how the Russians measure it today. When we stopped at the research laboratories, sometimes we would invite the scientists aboard and during lunch we would have such interesting conversations.

We visited the Chilean Research Station. The scientists were a group of young university students doing research during the summer break. A story told to us was that the director of the labs had to sign up for two years but at the end of the first year when the ship brings their supplies he refused to stay that second year and when they told him he had to do so . . . he burned down the labs. Now the students are doing their research while living in what I would call a shack. When these researchers were told that they were to come aboard they showered under cans with holes in them. The girls even put on makeup and where so beautiful that I will never forget them. They wanted to see my cabin and when they saw my bathroom they let out with these sighs and awes at what they would have given just to take a shower there. It was a new ship and beautifully decorated for an expedition ship and such a contrast to their shack. Just meeting research scientists like these young people who were enduring these hardships to help better this world made me have faith in the future of our environment.

I saw many species of penguins on that cruise. On the Falkland Islands, I saw the rock hopper penguins. They have these cute feathers coming out of their heads. I sat on the rocks with them and they just kept hopping by me. You should see they way they can hop onto the cliffs out of a raging sea of waves . . . it was an astounding sight. There were also crèches of their chicks where one of the adults would baby sit. I have a movie of the baby sitter nipping at this big albatross that went right through the middle of this crèche and scattered them. The "baby sitter" let that big bird know that he was mad.

The albatrosses were nesting on a cliff and there were hundreds of them. They had hatched many chicks and what a sight that was with the rock hoppers and the albatross on a beautiful sunny day. The scenery was breath taking.

We also stopped at South Georgia Island where we saw at least a million king penguins. There I sat on a whale vertebra—yes, it was that big—and my husband filmed those beautiful birds as I just enjoyed the interaction of those king penguins.

For all you lovers of Antarctica history we stopped at Grytviken, South Georgia and visited the grave of Sir Ernest Shackleton. For those of you who have never heard of him he was one the great adventurers of Antarctica. Many books have been written about his adventures. He was an Englishman and when he died, he requested that he be buried in Antarctica.

I know this next paragraph is not about penguins but I must tell you what I saw when we went ashore at Grytviken. We went ashore at an abandoned whaling station. The guide took us on a tour of huge chains and the biggest boiling pots I have ever seen. I was reminded of the cruelty of killing those whales. Now this is eerie—at that whaling station there was church among all this ruin. We heard organ music coming from it and when we checked it out there was one of the passengers (a famous German architect, Michael) playing the organ—it still worked. We all decided it was a tribute to Shackleton.

We went ashore at Falkland Island, where I saw gentoo penguins and maghellanic penguins. The maghellanic are the penguins you see at zoos. The gentoo penguin's bray like a jackass and called jackass penguins. We cruised further down the Paradise Peninsula where I saw chinstrap, and Adelie penguins that live closer to the South Pole.

SHACKLETON'S GRAVE AND NEARBY CHURCH

CHAPTER 2

Now that I have told you how I became so interested and intrigued with penguins, I must get on with my story of the Lords of Antarctica.

I had been writing this book long before the "March of the Penguins" was screened. I was devoting all my time to this book and editing the video. There is a coupon at the back of the book for the DVD. I hope you enjoy seeing the DVD after reading the book. I was especially happy to see the "March of the Penguins" because I shot my film the same year and in the same area. Yes, I was on the Ross Sea with landings at Cape Washington and Coulman Island. Fortunately, I was there during the height of summer—December. I was flown by helicopter from the ship close to the rookery at Cape Washington. It was a beautiful night. I shot my film from 7 PM to 1 AM with the best light a photographer could ask for filming. The sun was low (note the long shadows on the video) and there was no wind. Our naturalists who have been in Antarctica many times and were all professional photographers had never experienced such a night as this in Antarctica.

I must admit that wherever I have traveled I have had great weather and have the pictures to prove this is fact. You will notice the absence of wind at Cape Washington. I cannot say the same for Coulman Island where I left the sound of the wind on the video. There was hazy sunshine there at Coulman. At this stop, they garaged the ship at the edge of the ice. In other words, they secured the ship by ramming it into the ice field. We walked down a 25-step gangplank. I read where this island had one of the largest emperor rookeries. I did not see too many penguins but I was not up to tramping further into the island and was content to set up my camera and film close to the ship.

Now to the subject I love writing about—my emperor penguins and chicks. I have been studying everything written about the emperors. The emperor penguin ornithology name is Aptenodytes, forsteri that means wingless diver. They were named by two German naturalists who went with James Cook on his second voyage around the world in 1792-1795.

Thaddeus von Bellingshausen caught the first emperor penguin specimen in 1820. Antarctica was later discovered only because explorers were looking for the breeding colony of this amazing bird, whose hold on the world's imagination is still very alive. Robert Falcon Scott, historic for his adventures into Antarctica, set out in 1901 on board the S.S. Discovery to find the eggs of the emperor penguin. Scientist at that time thought the penguin was the most primitive bird on earth (which was not true) but they needed an embryo to understand the origin of the feathers. This is important because even the feathers of a penguin are made for water; their short, slightly curved feathers alternate and overlap like tiles on a roof. The tips are oily enough to repel water and keep the sea out. A mat of downy filaments grows from the shaft of each feather, forming with its neighbors a dense undershirt lying close to the skin. This traps a layer of warm air, and acts as additional waterproofing in case the outer layer of feather tips breaks down. The penguins are not as clumsy as they appear as they waddle along the ice, but in water, it is a completely different story, for they are in their element. Adult penguins spend 75 percent of their lives in the water, where they literally fly through the sea, using their wings in a different habitat. They are more at home in the water because they surrender their ability to soar through the air in order to "fly" through the water better. Their wings act the same while they are swimming as a bird does when it is flying. They are really flying under water. Emperors can exert propulsion on both the upstroke and down stroke while going through the water. Emperor penguins also zoom to a depth of 1,500 feet to feed. They do this by holding their breath for as long as 22 minutes.

Emperor penguins can live longer without breathing than people can because they store more oxygen in their muscles. There is more oxygen in cold water, which also helps them to breathe. They also conserve energy because their streamlined shapes and powerful wings allow them to swim through the water very efficiently. Emperor penguins can swim up to 8 miles per hour and will typically catch five to six fish before surfacing. They can even leap out of the water several feet to get away from the leopard seals or orcas whales that prey on them.

Long glides to the surface probably help emperor penguins conserve energy during their deepest dives. They have solid bones while sky bound birds have hollow bones to lighten their weight, penguins gradually lost that internal airspace—decreasing their buoyancy so they can dive to great depths.

The emperor penguin tolerates the outside air that is minus 20 to minus 30 degrees Fahrenheit. There is more than 60-degree temperature difference separated by a layer of feathers that is maybe a half an inch thick. This insulation is necessary because not only do emperor penguins rear their young in this extreme Antarctic environment—they do it while fasting. Once they hit the ice, there will be no opportunity to feed. They need the stability of the sea ice while they are breeding and rearing their chicks. This ice will melt during the summer. Starting in January their colony sites will begin breaking up into the open ocean. Remember the emperor's only source of food comes from the sea.

In the Antarctic, summer starts in December when the food is most available making it possible for their chicks to go to sea and fed. As the ice, starts breaking up the young chicks become anxious when they realize that their parents are not returning. The chicks then have to leave the rookery and venture into a dark and frigid sea. I have read that eight out of every 10 chicks do not survive. They become food for the leopard seals and orcas whales. They become part of the food chain just as the fish is the food for the penguin.

I do not like the skuas because they attack the baby chicks. Skuas are carnivores. There is a strange reaction to this happening by the emperor penguins. They do nothing to stop the attack of the skuas or protect their chicks. The skuas do not attack a crèche but will find a lonely chick that cannot defend its self. From what I have read, the chick does not cry out so the parent does not know if it is their chick and they are oblivious to a predator. Again, the chicks are part of the food chain this time for the skuas.

When the ice has melted and the chicks thermal feathers have grown in they join their parents and dive into the seas. Sometimes the chicks will ride on the same iceberg as their parents but it is not clear whether they are still a family. Nobody knows precisely what happens to the emperor chicks when they ride these ice floes. The chicks do not stay with their parents once they go to sea.

They spend four to five years at sea before they return to the rookery where they were born to find a mate and have their chicks. We do not know if a pair stays together at sea.

Emperor penguins are very curious and in my film at Coulman Island I had a group come ashore and toboggan up to that red and yellow thing with a camera that was me. I write about this later on.

Since adults do not return to the Antarctic ice shelves for months at a time. Where do they get the water they drink? At sea, penguins distill their own fresh water. To do this they have special nasal glands that lie embedded in the skull immediately above the eyes. It amazes me the adaptability these penguins have to exist in Antarctica.

It has been written that they make hundreds of dives a day, but they only spend about four hours a day diving. It has been assumed that the corpus striatum, rather than the cerebrum, is the seat of their being, and the brain, for all its great expansion, is concerned far more with keen sensory susceptibilities and delicate muscular coordination than with any processes that might properly be termed "mental." Why should a penguin need "brains" when its fundamental and inherited behavior pattern takes care of them through the seasonal cycle and the generations? This brings to mind the facts the females instinctively know when to return to the male and chick almost to the day the chick is hatched. Also, read that weather warnings make the emperors unsettled when they knew another terrific storm was brewing. The sky would be black and threatening, the barometer would begin to fall, and then snowflakes would drift onto the mountains upper heights. The explorers found observing the penguin's migration to the sea would serve them well as weather warnings.

Another amazing fact about their intuition is that they all know how to find their way back to the same rookery every mating season. They may come from different directions but go back to the rookery they knew as chicks. Just imagine emperors breeding in the Bay of Whales in the Ross Sea have been found with recognizable pebbles in their stomachs that could have come from a site more than 340 miles away, and the rookery itself can be another 100 miles from the sea. These penguins are preparing to mate and they are fasting because they are so far from the sea.

We do not know if the emperors are monogamous. I know some of the penguins species mate for life. The king penguin does but they also raise a chick for two years. Back to the emperors—we do not know if they look for last year's mate. They come from the sea in single file, one behind the other. When they arrive at the rookery, they begin a search for a partner. There are more females then males which can make this an interesting time for the males as the females will interfere with a couple—they are not violent just a lot of slapping of wings. This shortage of males could be because some of the males incubating the eggs do not survive the fasting and storms for the long wait for the female to return.

The emperor penguins have a very polite society. Nobody bothers anyone else and yet they are not isolated. In extreme weather conditions it is imperative that they join together or freeze separately. There can be up to ten thousand birds assembled in a rookery. To keep from freezing to death they form huddles. This huddle is a large circle where males crowd together thus the name huddle (the French call it a tortue). They are rotating from the center to the outside of the circle so that when the storms come they can move in close to one another, shoulder to shoulder. This helps them to survive in this extreme cold. The middle of the huddle is unusually warm and one would think that every penguin would fight to be at the epicenter of warmth. However, penguin etiquette requires that no penguin seek to advance himself at the expense of another and that way every emperor will benefit. The chicks also instinctively form these huddles when they have bad weather while they are in the crèches. Can you see humans looking out like that for our fellow man? I think not.

They do consider the weather a factor when they choose the rookeries. They go where a mountain will break the winds. Two factors in choosing the rookery is the following; one it has to be where the ice will not melt while they are raising their chicks and two where they can get some protection from the cruel winter winds that blow in July and August.

We learn in the mating ritual of the emperor penguin the male or female will approach the other and slowly lowers his or her head with a loud sigh. A short song follows this, while the courting penguin keeps it beak pointing vertically down. The other penguin lifts its head and they listen intently. They face each other and are completely still for thirty to forty seconds. Suddenly one of the birds will incline his or her head and begin to sing again, which causes the other to follow suit. That is it. Either they separate and continue the same ritual with another penguin, or they follow one another, a deal having been struck. They then walk off together, puff up their necks and do an exaggerated swagger. Finding a partner can take anywhere from a couple of hours to a couple of days.

Often the pair will become separated when it is cold and they join huddles. They invariably find each other again, often without any vocalization with them all looking alike, this could be a formable task. The birds themselves do not have any such problem.

The emperors usually wait for good weather to copulate, any time between April 10 and June 6. They separate themselves from the rest of the colony and face each other, remaining still for a time. The male bends his head down and contacts his abdomen, and shows the female the spot on his belly where he has a flap of skin that serves as a pouch for the egg and baby chick. This is a fold of loose abdominal skin, a bare (the lack of feathers facilitates the flow of heat) to keep the egg and chick warm. This brooding patch wraps over the egg to form a warm brood cavity. This act causes the female to do the same. Their heads touch, and the male bends his head down to touch the female's pouch. Both begin to tremble visibly. The female lies face down on the ice, partially spread her wings and opens her legs. The male climbs on her back and they mate for ten to thirty seconds.

Afterwards they stay together constantly, leaning against one another when they are standing up. About a month later, between May 1 and June 12 the female lays a single greenish-white egg. For sixteen years of observation the annual date, which the colony's first egg was laid, varied by only eight days. The egg weighs almost a pound. This is one of the largest eggs of any bird. I held an egg on the trip when an ornithologist found an abandoned egg. They have had success in the past in producing chicks from such eggs.

The male stays by the female's side, his eyes fixed on her pouch. As soon as he sees the egg, he sings, a variation of what has been called "ecstatic display" by early observers. The male penguin performs this call with his head and wings raised. She too takes up the melody. She catches the egg and places it on her feet. Both penguins sing in unison staring at the egg for an hour then the female slowly walks around the male, who gently touches the egg on her feet with his beak, making soft groans, his whole body trembling. He shows the female his pouch. Gently she puts the egg down on the ice and just as gently he rolls it with his beak between his large, black, powerfully clawed feet, and with great difficulty places the egg onto the surface of his feet. He rests back on his heels so that his feet make the least contact with the ice. The transfer of the egg is a delicate operation. If it falls on the ice and rolls away it can freeze in minutes or it might be stolen. If it is snatched away by a female penguin who failed to find a mate, it chances of survival are slight because the intruder will eventually abandon the egg, since she has no mate to relieve her. She must eventually go to sea to feed.

With the egg transfer successfully completed, the happy couple both sing. The male parades about in front of the female, showing her his pouch with the egg inside. This thick fold, densely feathered on the outside and bare inside, barely covers the egg and keeps it at about 95 degrees even when the temperature falls to 95 degrees below zero. The female begins to back away, each time a little farther. He tries to follow her, but it is hard, since he is balancing the egg. Suddenly she is gone, moving purposefully toward the open sea. The other females in the colony, who, by the end of May or June, have all left for the ocean, join her. The females have fasted for nearly a month and a half, and have lost anywhere between 17 to 30 percent of their total weight. They do not have the extra fat of 30 pounds that the male had put on during the summer and she is in desperate need of food.

The female must renew her strength and vitality so that she can return with food for her chick. When she goes to the sea, she takes the shortest route to reach open water surround by ice. Penguins appear to be able to navigate by the reflection of the clouds on the water, using what has been called a "water sky."

The male penguin, who has also been fasting, is now left with the egg balanced on his feet. The first egg was laid on the first of May; the chick will be born in August. Since the seasons are reversed south of the equator, full winter has arrived, with the violent blizzards and the lowest temperatures of the year. The emperor penguins are well adapted to the coldest climate in the world that has 24 hours of Antarctic nights. Their plumage is waterproof, windproof, flexible, and renewed annually. They also have the aforementioned huddles to help them survive this bitter cold. The males are passive and know the long fast is ahead of them. They have fasted for 2 months and now face another 2 months of fasting. Moving about with the egg balanced on their feet is difficult at the best of times.

Sometimes a few restless males with eggs on their feet go out into the frozen countryside. Whether it is 4 miles or 1mile, they always manage to return through thick snow, their eggs precariously balanced. It is a rare hardy penguin that ventures out into a bad storm. However, there is always a few that do. They no longer walk but lie on their bellies and using their wings to toboggan themselves forward keeping the egg pressed against the incubating pouch with their feet. I am amazed that they can move about like this with the egg.

Even an injured bird will continue to protect his egg. One penguin had a bad wound on his foot that did not permit him to stand up. He kept apart from the other birds and managed to keep his egg balanced on his single good foot even without standing. Birds have been known to fall over small precipices, roll down snowy slopes, trip over rocks, tumble heavily on slippery bare ice, or navigate their way among very rough ridges of hard snow and still have his egg. This fact proves that the first concern of the male emperor is for his egg. One of the reasons I have such a respect for the emperor penguins is that they put the future of their species before their own existence. The human male is notorious for abandoning his offspring, which has always truly concerned me for those children raised without their fathers or parental love. This example shows what the emperor penguins accomplish and endure at such great odds . . . to preserve their species.

I love the way they waddle, like we humans they walk upright. Don't you love the way they waddle? Just to tell you how smart those ornithologists studying them are they concluded that the side-to-side movement is to help them conserve energy, which amounted to 80 percent of the mechanical energy required for walking. This was quite high because other measurements for humans and other birds have found they only recovered up to 70 percent of the mechanical energy. Unbelievably the penguin waddle is more efficient than a human's walk . . . I do not think humans would be called cute if they waddle.

The waddle is like an "inverted pendulum" effect and it compares to a wobbling bowling pin. Kinetic energy and gravity combine to keep it rocking back and forth over its center of gravity. The penguins also waddle backward and forward.

Another fact I wish to convey is the belly of the emperors is white so when he is swimming it is hard for the predators to see them when they look up. The black back also makes it difficult to see them from above the water.

I must mention that the call the parents and chicks make to find each other is very unique because each family has its own call. No two families have the same call. To me this becomes a penguin symphony and you will hear this sound all through the video. I love this sound of the penguins.

The adult penguin will only feed his or her own chick. They probably only have enough food for a single chick. Remember they regurgitate what fish they catch and they do not have a big capacity to store this food and feed another chick. It takes two parents to feed their hungry chick. The chick has to get its full growth so it can live on its own after December.

The adult penguins do not fear we humans as they are very much like us. They walk upright as we do, are very vocal, have families, form huddles to keep warm and are social just like us.

These emperor penguins live in the coldest climate in the world. They survive and raise their chicks with tenderness. You will see in the video the parent's never once even flip the hungry, demanding chick when they are begging. I love the way they shake their heads. It is so human. I hope you have learned to love the penguins for more than that they are cute and that you love the way they waddle.

On with my journal of the adventure of a lifetime.

CHAPTER 3

My family questioned me about taking this long journey alone. Why go back to Antarctica when you had already been there? To see the emperor penguins was my answer.

The flight to Australia was a long one. You never check your camera equipment or notebook through so I had to carry it on board. Believe me it was heavy. My workouts at the gym really paid off when it came to being a photographer and lugging the equipment. At my age the three-times-a-week workout with the 100 lb weights proved to be worth the effort it took. You don't think about this need for strength but you sure need it when you are tramping around in the Antarctic with photo equipment

I flew out of LAX International Airport on the Sunday after Thanksgiving and I have never been in such a mass of humanity. They were all shipping huge boxes with them. I could hardly get through the airport without dodging these boxes. I allowed the usual two hours ahead of time but most people must have allowed longer because there was not one seat available to wait for boarding. It was an exhausting wait until we boarded the plane. The agent at the counter was kind to me and gave me one of three seats making it possible to sleep. I got all cozy with my pillow and blanket as we took off. I was ready to fall a sleep when the steward brings a father and his 4-year-old son to claim the two seats. At this distance it is very tiring having to sit up and sleep. At that time I was reminded that I had enough frequent flier miles to up-grade and could not use them because the airline wouldn't give that advantage on short notice. This does not bode well when there were a lot of empty seats in business and first class.

There was a short flight from Melbourne to Hobart, Tasmania. The passengers for the cruise were all booked in a hotel at the docks. We were greeted by the leaders of our cruise and given our cabin assignments. It was time to meet my roommate for the cruise.

This was a new experience for me to share a cabin with a complete stranger. Fortunately it turned out fine. She was from the Netherlands and to her joy she found there were six other passengers from her country. She had her own group of friends among those fellow Dutch passengers, and they conversed in their language and hung out together.

We had free time in Hobart, so two of us booked a tour of Tasmania. I wanted to at least see where the fairy penguin's rookery was located. They are nocturnal so all that I saw was the holes on the beach that were their nests. The sand was covered with their footprints.

I was also interested in the island because some of the original settlers of the island were Clifford's. We met Lord Clifford in England who was born there. They were the major landowners and ranchers. Also spoke with the Clifford Company that builds catamaran ferries that have become popular in Europe and the Orient.

The countryside was beautiful and many different species of plants I had never seen before. Australia is unique in its flora and fauna. The landscapes were beautiful. Not many people have settled outside of Hobart so it is wide open with rolling hills and lakes. We had lunch at restaurant that was part of a family's home. It was an opportunity to speak with the locals.

TASMANIAN COUNTRYSIDE

CHAPTER 4

Kapitan Khlebnikov, the ship, was arriving from Cape Town, South Africa and had run into hurricane force winds and in going around them we were delayed a day in our departure. While waiting, Quark took us on a tour of Hobart. We learned the history of the town. The little zoo especially fascinated us with the native animals found only in Australia. Hobart and Tasmania and are quite a contrast to the other cities and islands I have seen throughout my travels. There are very large experimental laboratories for their work and studies in connection with the preservation of the environment in Antarctica. There are research labs on Macquarie Island. Remember this island when I write about it later. Australia and New Zealand have many restrictions for preserving nature especially in Antarctica. We had to disinfect our boots whenever we left the ship. This was also done when we came back aboard.

KAPITAN KHLEBNIKOV

HOBART, TASMANIA
Day 2 Thursday, December 4, 2003

We boarded the ship and I was assigned cabin 519. It was on deck 5. This was the same deck I was assigned on the Arctic cruise. Now when you travel into what you know can be rough seas the lower the deck the smoother the ride. The cabins are very sufficient and my roommate was very compatible about storing our things in the cabin. When you travel to Antarctica it requires a lot of warm clothes. These clothes are bulky to store and the space in the cabins is limited but again my cabin mate and I worked out the sharing of the storage. Fortunately I own a whole wardrobe of cold weather clothes. These were collected during my skiing and snowmobile holidays.

My cabin mate showered at night and I showered in the morning. It's the details like this that need to be decided when you share with a stranger. We were quite a contrast in personalities. This was part of the adventure sharing a cabin with a stranger and it was not a problem.

HOBART HARBOR

TASMANIAN RESEARCH ENVIRONMENTAL CENTER

I was familiar with the Kapitan Khlebnikov from my Arctic cruise and knew it had been a working ship. It was very comfortable and the cabins were accommodating. My roommate was an intensive care nurse who suffered from motion sickness so she took the bunk that we called the cradle and my bunk was called the rocking chair. All of the bunks have railings, straps and handlebars to hold onto when the sea really gets rough.

It was an international group of passengers. Ten countries were represented. The crew was Russian and spoke little English. My cabin maid and I wanted to learn each other's language so we practiced on each other. She was such fun. She was young and pretty and kept my cabin in excellent condition. When traveling I always use the printouts of the language of the country or ship that you are on. Quark always provides a page of words for limited conversation. Not being a linguist lots of times we would laugh over my futile attempts to have a conversation. I would suggest to you who travel to make this effort to communicate because the person with whom you are speaking appreciates it. The main attempts made are the AM and PM greetings, please and thank you. Please is Pajaloosta. Thank you is Spaseeba—this is fun to say—try it. On a previous cruise where there were multi-national passengers I greeted a Taiwanese in Japanese, he smiling corrected me so you do have to know your nationalities. We greeted one another for the rest of the cruise in Taiwanese.

If you recall the ship was a day late due to the hurricane they had to go around. Those rough seas were with us as we headed across the Tasmanian Sea. The Tasmanian Sea is one of the roughest seas in the world.

A description of the structure of an icebreaker needs to be explained. It is not like other ships. It is built to handle a sea of ice. First of all it has tremendous engines with 24,000 horsepower. This is needed to force this huge hull on top of the ice and creating a crack. They then follow this crack as it opens up and the ship goes on its way. I show this in the video. The hull is massive and rounded so the ice does not cling to it. There are no projections for the ice to get hung up on the hull. They run water down over the hull while cruising in ice so the ice will not stick to the sides and build up. This shape of the ship makes for more movement in waves causing a lot of rock and rolling. With the rough seas we had encountered my arms became bruised from being thrown up against the walls. Using the bathroom was especially tough when putting my makeup on—it actually had me laughing. Sometimes I wonder at my vanity that looking good was that important. I had to hang on to the handlebar while showering. The bathrooms are not large and it is a good thing when you are sailing through rough seas. By the 5th day it became a little trying.

Now you must remember this cruise is in some of the roughest seas in the world. It is called the South Sea and becomes the Antarctic Ocean. I am truly amazed how capable the crew is dealing with these rough seas and serving us. Once I got my sea legs I was then able to move about the ship with no problems. I love the sea and can tolerate these rough seas. I felt sorry for those who did get seasick. The doctor on board had a special seasick medication.

Along with this rough sea were the howling winds. I did not venture out on the deck much. I am not very big and the winds blew me about the deck. Besides the wind blowing made me cold.

CHAPTER 5

There are lots of things to do on board the ship. There is an auditorium where we would meet for lectures and instructions. We would have at least two lectures or instructions for keeping us safe from harm a day.

We had international famous lecturers. It was rewarding to attend these sessions because there is so much to learn about what I would be seeing. The expedition staff was outstanding and the following is a description of their backgrounds and credentials.

Susan Adie was our Expedition Leader. Susan was very organized and friendly as she herded us about with the help of her staff. Susan for 25 years has been guiding trips on marine biology trips. She has led groups for National Geographic Society (USA), Smithsonian Institution, and American Museum of Natural History, the Explorers Club and National Audubon Society. We were very fortunate to have her expertise.

Tim Soper was our Assistant Expedition Leader. He earned an honors degree in Ocean Science at the University of Wales, Bangor. Studying a combination of Marine Biology and Oceanography. Voyages in the last eight years have taken him to every continent and across every ocean and into the ice at both ends of the earth. His father, Tony Soper was aboard as our ornithologist. Tony is an avid naturalist and filmmaker and co-founded the BBC's famous Natural History Unit and became its first film producer. He has a great speaking voice and narrates programs for British National Geographic. Tony has enjoyed exploring the Antarctic for the last ten seasons. He has crossed the Drake Passage over 100 times and has sailed the seven seas and circled the world three times. Tony has written numerous books that are too many to mention but you now have his name so you might pursue finding his books in your local libraries.

TONY SOPER

TIM SOPER

Frank Todd, our prominent biologist is an authority particularly known for his studies of the sea birds of Antarctica. He is considered one of today's leading aviculturalists. Frank has devoted fifteen years to the highly published "Penguin Encounter" project. He was the first to be successful at breeding penguins outside of their native habitat and the first breeding colony of emperor penguins beyond the Antarctic. He actually brought home an abandoned emperor egg that he will hatch. When handling the egg I was surprised how heavy it was. Frank lives in San Diego, California and is the person who made the penguins at Sea World famous. He was awarded the Bean Award the highest award of the American Association of Zoological Parks and Aquariums in 1980, 1981, and 1983. He is currently the Executive Director of Ecocepts International. He has also been awarded the United State Polar Medal for Scientific Service in the Antarctic (NSF).

Rod Ledingham was our Geologist. He was born in the north of Scotland and in his youth he spent his spare time mountaineering and skiing. Rod graduated from Aberdeen University where he studied glacial geomorphology. Rod joined the British Antarctic Survey as meteorologist on the Antarctic Peninsula. In 1978 Rod was working as a field assistant to a geologist when a plane crash on the Antarctic plateau left him and four others stranded. He spent a second year at Fossil Bluff until they were rescued at the end of the year. He entertained us with a film of this adventure with great humorous commentaries. I suggested he write a book.

Brad Stahl was a naturalist and a graduate of Cornell University. He has worked for several years leading snorkeling trips in the British and US Virgin Islands, guiding passengers in the Pacific Northwest, and Alaska. Most recently in the Amazon and Antarctica. Brad is currently constructing a replica of 1800's 170-foot wooden three-masted merchant schooner for the Salem Maritime Museum. It will be classified as a national historic site when completed at its homeport, Salem, MA. Susan and Brad are husband and wife that not only sail together as leaders of expeditions but own an environmental education firm that specializes in providing educational opportunities for schools.

Lorne Kriwoken was called upon to be our historian as the man schedule to do so was injured and was unable to continue on the voyage. He informed us of all the rules and regulations concerning the environment. He made the rather sleep provoking information about all the environmental laws and restrictions as entertaining as possible. Lorne is a teacher and his students are fortunate to have such a lively educator. He was also our photographer of passengers for our logbook.

One of the things with expedition cruising with Quark is the camaraderie between the Expedition Staff and the passengers. We sat together at lunch and dinner and got to know each other. Do realize there were just 73 passengers and many were not fluent in English. There was a group from Taiwan that did not speak English and their little interpreter who spoke fluent English celebrated her 21st birthday while on the cruise.

I would also like to mention the other workers on the ship and that was Danielle Sogno who was the shop manager and served in the dining room. We had some great conversations. She was a lot of fun. She also appreciated my purchases in her little shop. Then there was our pretty Nordic (can't recall if she was Norwegian or Swedish) Elke Fraider, the bartender. All the waitresses and busboys were very friendly because everyone loves being in Antarctica. Also people who do this kind of cruising are interesting to converse with, especially the discussions on what we were seeing.

CHAPTER 6

There are no polar bears in Antarctica. That is the first thing people ask me when they hear about the cruise to Antarctica. I investigated the naming of Antarctica, an Egyptian geographer, Ptolemy called it Terra Australi Incognita, the Unknown Southern. Two thousand years earlier Aristotle agreed with others that the world was round and that a great landmass must exist far to the south to balance those lands in the north. The Greeks charted the northern constellation of the great bear Arctos and named the north Arctica. It then became logical that the southern sky would contain a polar complement called "anti-arctos" which we now call Antarctica. That is why it is now known as Antarctica.

Let's go through the itinerary of the cruise. There was the time spent in Hobart. We are now at sea and it is Friday the 5th of December. The air temperature is 52 degrees and the sea temperature is 59 degrees Fahrenheit. We had a full day at sea. After breakfast Tony Soper, showed us slides of the SEABIRDS OF THE SOUTHERN OCEAN introducing many of the species we would be seeing. We were also told that we would be crossing the Antarctic Convergence. This sea is among the stormiest of the planet and also the most productive in terms of biomass, sustaining very large populations of petrels, seals and whales.

For the birders on this cruise they spent a lot of time on deck filming all these rare species. One of my favorite birds is the albatross. On my prior cruise to the Falkland Islands I saw a cliff just white with these beautiful birds. They are one of the largest species of birds. They have an eight-foot wingspan. We were told that they travel great distances by gliding. The birds follow the ship because the churning up of the water brings a lot of sea life to the surface. They have a feast.

MAP ROUTE

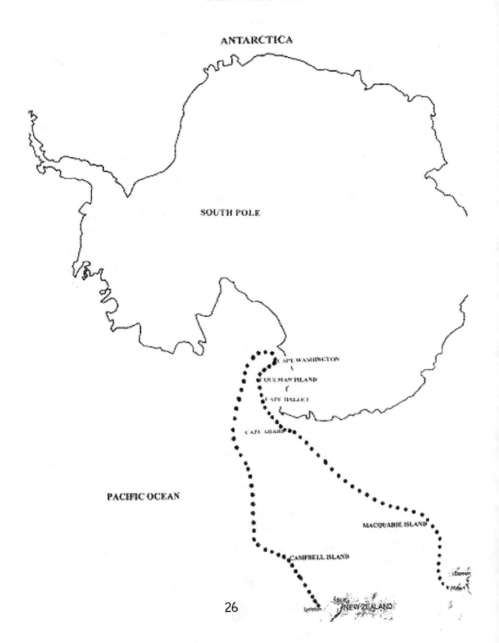

ANTARCTICA

SOUTH POLE

CAPE WASHINGTON

COULMAN ISLAND

CAPE HALLET

CAPE ADARE

PACIFIC OCEAN

MACQUARIE ISLAND

CAMPBELL ISLAND

NEW ZEALAND

AT SEA
Day 3 Friday, December 5, 2003

Latitude/Longitude:	45°29'S, 147°52'E
Wind:	W, 29 knots
Air Temperature:	11°C/52°F
Sea Temperature:	15°C/59°F

Quark Expeditions gave us parkas and it was quite a scene everyone trying to find the right size. These parkas are a requirement for this cruise. Packing for this cruise was quite a challenge for me because of having to pack heavy warm clothes and I took Ugg and rubber boots. I wanted to bring the parka home so I gave my boots to a young New Zealand scientist that we picked up from a research base in Antarctica—they (he gave the Uggs to his girlfriend) were very grateful. At home I gave one of my grandsons the parka for his snow boarding trips.

Our first orientation and lecture was with Lorne Kriwoken, he was our historian. He lectured about the importance of the port we passed on our tour of Hobart. Hobart is very involved in Antarctic science. There is a complex of very new and modern laboratories that were impressive. Australia and New Zealand are very much involved in the conservation of Antarctica.

After lunch Frank Todd, our Marine Biologist, gave a lecture called OCEAN WONDERS. It was about the soft-plumaged Petrels and the Black-browed and Wondering Albatross. He showed us stunning pictures of these and other ocean wonderers. Courtship and nest behavior were discussed. As I mentioned earlier I had seen these nested colonies among the rock hopper rookery in the Falklands. To quote Frank it is "controlled chaos in landings" at the nest colonies.

The albatross name is an English sailor's corruption of the Portuguese ancestral for a pelican, a bird that early explorers would have known from the Mediterranean. Albatrosses are divided into two genera, DIOMEDEA and PHOEBEDTRIA. There are14 species and they are commonly known as "Great Albatrosses"—the Wandering and Royal. Small albatrosses are better known to be mollymawks, from the Dutch Mal, foolish and mok for gull. Another name for them is "gooney" from the English dialect word for simpleton. These pejorative and richly undeserved epithets are because when you see the albatross ashore, out of their element they appear clumsy and partly because of their endearing but ill-advised innocence in standing quietly while being bludgeoned by a club and taken for the pot. There is a disastrous population decline that is clearly attributable to the long line fishing industry.

In the late 18th and 19th centuries, albatrosses were much persecuted both for their meat and their plumage. Sailors used hook and line to catch them and make pouches out of their webbed feet, feather rugs from their skins, and pipe stems from their bones.

CHAPTER 7

During these days on the open sea those of us who could tolerate the heavy seas would congregate in the lounge when we were not going to lectures. There was a library with excellent books that educated us about all the wonderful things we would be seeing. The books we all enjoyed most were those written by our staff. There were beautiful photographic books brought on board by our world-renowned professional photographers. There were 8 professional photographers on board. They were from all over the world such as Cape Town, South Africa, England, Germany, Holland, Japan and three from United States. They were there to film the emperor penguins. They sell their pictures for calendars, greetings cards and as works of art. They also wrote books with their pictures for publishing. Everyone loves penguins. The scenery was so beautiful. Of course they filmed the seals, whales and all those gorgeous birds.

One day when we were no longer going ashore but heading to New Zealand in open water they put together a showing of photographs that people had taken during the trip. This is when digital is really useful. You not only can see how your camera and technique is working but also work with editing on the computers that all the photographers brought with them. Most of the photographers and that was everyone on board used still cameras.

My roommate suffered from motion sickness and she took medicine that made her sleepy so rather than disturb her I would take my notebook and disk out to the lounge to view my work and I was always joined by some of the passengers. Those that were in the lounge especially loved the sounds of my penguins and the begging of the chicks. If only humans could be as patient with there babies as these adult penguin parents. These poor chicks have to get their growth in just six months because once they go to sea and leave their parents they are on their own.

A lot of the passengers requested that they be sent a DVD of these penguins when it was edited. As I mentioned earlier about buying my latest Sony Digital 300 Handycam little did I know that it would be so difficult to edit my movie. The pictures were edited but I was unable to add my title or narration. My daughter saved me by editing and producing the film.

CHAPTER 8

AT SEA

Day 4 Saturday, December 6, 2003

Latitude/Longitude:	49°42'S, 150°39'E
Wind:	SW 29 knots
Air Temperature:	10°C/50°F
Sea Temperature:	10°C/50°F

We had eight Australians from their Hobart Research Center on the way to Macquarie Island. They are stationed there for 18 months and the ship transports them back and forth when it cruises there. Living aboard the ship is quite a contrast to their life on the island. You can imagine 7 course meals served on white linen and china in contrast to the habitat of a research station. There was a hilarious performance by the staff as they decontaminated everyone's outer field clothing in preparation for the landings, and vacuuming all backpacks to make sure no unwanted seeds reached Macquarie.

Thank goodness that the Kapitan Khleknikov was a big old strong ship. It is not pretty but ohhh so warm and comfortable. What the sailors of old would have given for this comfort on their trying adventures in these same waters.

When sailing on this same ship in the Arctic we cut through 12 feet of ice at Hell's Gate. It was smooth but noisy. On this cruise we experienced much more motion from the stormy seas than we encountered in the Arctic. Needless to say the South Ocean and Antarctic Sea live up to being called the roughest seas in the World. We really appreciated the five days we spent in the pack ice where the ship was stabilized by the ice.

The passengers seem to cope with this rocking and rolling. We went to lectures and read. There were 3 other passengers that made the foursome for bridge during those days at sea. We always had tea at 4:00 PM and with Austrian Chef you can imagine what pastries his staff made for us.

The food was so delicious and when you are hiking about in the snow and cold you burn up a lot of calories. It was a great opportunity for me to indulge my love of food. The desserts with dinner were delicious until my clothes became tighter and that was my signal to pass up the goodies for a while.

CHAPTER 9

APPROACHING MACQUARIE ISLAND
Day 5 Sunday, December 7, 2003

Latitude/Longitude:	53°30'S, 157°49'E
Wind:	31 knots
Air Temperature:	6°C/43°F
Sea Temperature:	9°C/48°F

It is a lively day at sea with 10-foot waves. We are within 60 nautical miles of Macquarie Island and Susan called a lecture to advise us about the guidelines of the International Association of Antarctica Tour Operators (IAATO) which will govern our activities on shore. We were given a briefing on zodiac landings. Zodiacs made it possible to make landings on remote beaches and rocky shores which are pretty much impossible for conventional boats. Believe me, there have been some pretty exciting landings.

Rod Ledingham, our Staff Field Operations, entertained us with how not to dress for our disembarkation to great laughter and applause. Then Lorne showed us how to be properly dressed.

At midday we sighted Macquarie Island in bright sunshine. The sun illuminated a wild sea of galloping horses (this is Tony's description) hurling crashing waves over the bridge. Now this bridge is on the 9th deck so let your imagination picture that scene. We approached on the lee side and found there was a heavy line of surf along the beach. The wind actually increased with gusts up to 50 knots. There were plans to land these Aussies at the Australian station at Buckle Bay but that was impossible so the ship proceeded to Sandy Bay. Here conditions were no better, but Susan had two scouts Brad (her husband) and Tim that craned two scout zodiacs into the water from the heli deck and took two of the Aussie team to scout the possibility of a landing. With binoculars we watched from the bridge as they worked their way along the coast. We could clearly see the King penguins on the beach and the Royal penguin colonies higher up on the slopes. Our scouts tried four different beaches and found them all marginally possible, in spite of frequent williwaws.

The real problem was disembarking from the ship, as the Kapitan Khlebnikov's roll was alternately putting the gangway stage well in and out of the sea. We watched as they loaded the supplies for the base (this was there first delivery of the summer) and they really needed the food supplies. Plus the fact we had our guests, the rangers and scientists to drop off. When we reached the island to take them ashore it was like horror movie setting. It was almost like the island was rejecting them. Never-the-less—they had to go ashore by zodiac because the winds were too strong for the helicopters to land. I was very impressed with the courage of these men to face those raging weather elements. It takes rugged men on this rugged island. They had to take 7 men ashore. There were 2 men returning. They were Martin and John. I watched in disbelief that these men and zodiacs would struggle against the sea, winds and survive. Yes, we have modern equipment and modes of travel but the KINGS OF THE WIND AND SEA ARE STILL ALL POWERFUL.

I must tell you about my conversation with Martin, the Australian from Macquarie Island. The first time I met with Martin he asked where was I from and when I told him California—"he said did you vote for Arnold?" (with accent). Can you believe that this man living on this isolated island for 18 months had watched television and was concerned about my vote? You go to places like Antarctica to get away from life in Southern California and here I am confronted with politics. The world is getting much smaller with all our satellites and electronics.

Macquarie Island is an unusual island because there is evidence of the rock types found in the oceanic crust that extends from the upper mantle, approximately, 4 miles below the sea floor, to the rocks that are currently forming on the sea floor. This formation is typical of mid-oceanic ridge environments where new crust is being formed, providing evidence for plate tectonics and continental drift. It is the only island in the world composed entirely of oceanic crust.

In addition, Macquarie Island represents spectacular steep escarpments: extensive peat beds: large numbers of lakes, tarns, and pools: and extensive congregations of wildlife, including Royal and King penguins, Elephant seals, and four species of albatross. At 1515, Captain Vasil'yev took the ship on to

Lusitania Bay, where the beach was crowded to bursting with king penguins. This part of the island was strictly out of bounds for visitors, so there was no question of landing, but we did get a pretty good view of a large rookery of penguins. Even though we were off the coast you could still smell as Frank our expert called it a "heavenly effluvium." I have been to a king penguin rookery where the smell from guano is so strong that it burnt my nose. Now the king penguins are the only species of penguins that have this heavenly effluvium (love that description). The emperors or Adelies did not smell. I was told the reason for this is the king penguin diet of fish is pure protein. Also there are not enough heavy rains in Antarctica to wash away the guano from these rookeries where there were at least a million penguins. Actually at one time they used to gather this guano and ship it for fertilizer. It was very valuable because it was so rich in nutrients. Seabird feces are rich in organic nitrogen and phosphate: which encourages a lush growth of grasses and flowering plants. In wet climates, these droppings are soon leached of their mineral richness, but on tropical coasts (little recorded rain) they desiccate to become potentially commercial crop. Guano is an Inca word for the naturally desiccated dung of fish-eating seafowl such as cormorants, boobies, pelican, and tropical penguins. The Incas protected the birds and extracted the guano on a sensible basis, taking it at a rate slower than it was produced. However they no longer do this because it was harmful procedure at the rookeries. Later harvesters were not so enlightened, killing the golden goose with the usual enthusiasm. During the 19th century, guano was a major product of international trade. Between 1848 and 1875, more than 20 million tons were shipped to Europe and the United States by way of square-riggers from Valparaiso. In the early 20th century, the deposits began to fail, with dire effects on the Peruvian economy. From 1909, a more sensible policy was pursued and guano was treated as a crop instead of limitless resource. The seabird islands became sanctuaries, with walled defenses against pests: the situation stabilized and improved. Now a new danger threatens, as the possibility of large-scale harvesting of plankton endangers the seabirds' hunting grounds. I learned on my previous cruise that the Japanese discovered that krill was very high in protein and they canned it for human consumption. It tasted like tuna and was a very popular. That was stopped when it was discovered that a whole island of penguins starved to death because they no longer had their krill.

At 1730, the Kapitan Khlebnikov closed the bay and drifted, holding position for 40 minutes while two inflatables came from the base to collect the party of scientists that had been with us since sailing from Hobart, plus five loads of baggage and assorted equipment, including a guitar and Didgeridoo (an Australian aboriginal horn). Now this unloading was in addition to the fore mentioned taking ashore of the base supplies.

At 1845, the last was offloaded and our two zodiacs repositioned to the afterdeck in order to leave the foredeck clear and ready for whatever the sea had to offer over the next few days. Remember we are still in the roughest seas in the world. Sadly, without our visit to either station or penguin's beaches, we regretfully cleared Macquarie and sailed south toward the ice. The next cruise had beautiful sunshine and friendly seas and they did go ashore. I have never seen the Royal penguins and had I hoped to see all 17 species of penguins.

CHAPTER 10

AT SEA

Day 6 Monday, December 8, 2003

Latitude/Longitude:	57°6'S, 161°31'E
Wind:	W, 31 knots
Air Temperature:	4°C/39°F
Sea Temperature:	4°C/39°F

The Kapitan Khlebnikov achieved a 40-degree roll during the night and we were enjoying a moderate swell and only an occasional 30-degree roll. The day was sunny with assorted petrels in our wake, plus black-footed albatross. I mentioned earlier that the birds follow the ship because the wake brings up a lot of the sea life to the surface making a feast for the birds. Photographers were so happy with this fact.

One of the things they had on the cruise was an Artist-in-Residence that introduced us to the Quark Polar Arts Programme and encouraged us to look at the many works that were exhibited in stairway wells and odd bulkheads around the ship. It is to remind us of the historic significance of artists who sailed with exploration expeditions from the earliest days with, for instance, Cook, D'Urville, Ross, and Nordenskjold. The work of Joseph Hooker and Edward Wilson has stood the test of time. I wonder if the same can be said for Kodachrome! Ove Altmann was our artist in residence and was in charge of the Quark Polar Arts Program. This is the inaugural year and it was very impressive the number of passengers that joined his classes. They were accomplished artists. My artistic talent is nil so I just enjoyed seeing the work of the talented shipmates . . .

Lorne, our Historian, spoke to us about the AUSTRALIAN WORLD HERITAGE AREAS: Jewels of the Crown. Under the 1972 World Heritage

Convention, World Heritage Areas (WHAs) are designated to conserve natural and cultural areas of outstanding universal values. Worldwide there are 754 natural and cultural properties (582 cultural and 149 natural). Only 23 WHA's represent both mixed natural and cultural values. Macquarie was declared an Australian WHA in 1997.

Out on the open decks the wind howled and the temperature dropped because we were entering the Antarctic Convergence. The Antarctica Convergence is the circumpolar region, conveniently drawn as a line undulating between 50° and 60°'S, it is well defined by thermometer readings—it is sometimes marked by a localized belt of fog or mist—where the warm, more saline surface currents coming south from the tropics meet the cold, denser, and less saline waters moving north from the Antarctic. The conflicting currents clash, converge, and sink. The mixing waters provide a sympathetic environment for an abundance of plankton, which nourishes huge numbers of seabirds and sea mammals.

CHAPTER 11

AT SEA

Day 7 Tuesday, December 9, 2003

Latitude/Longitude:	61°59'S, 165°38'N
Wind:	SW, 38 knots
Air Temperature:	-2°C/28°F
Sea Temperature:	0°C/32°F

During the night we crossed the Convergence, entered the biological Antarctic, and were now in cold waters. We are still pursuing a southeasterly course. We sighted our first large iceberg at 61°52'S 165°22'E.

The winds have picked up to 40 knots plus. This makes it difficult to walk against the wind on deck. It is cozy and warm inside the ship. You can look out the windows to see the beauty without the cold wind. Now all those who suffer from motion sickness can relax because we have sailed into the 2/10 pack ice and the rolling of the ship was much reduced—in fact it was a steady ride until we reached Cape Washington. Snow Petrels and Antarctic Petrels were keeping station with the ship. Minke whales had also been seen. You only find Snow Petrels in association with pack ice and always south of 55° latitude. They are sedentary birds, never straying far from their home base. Interesting facts is that when they return to the nest sites in November they may dig through three feet of snow to find the ground. Their main food is krill, small fish, and carrion taken on the wing in tern-style, but they will also forage for larger plankton animals from the edge older pack ice. This was an exciting day for me because we saw our first emperor penguin on an ice floe. Several more followed. Tabular icebergs came into view.

There is a sad history of the early exploration and importance of penguins as a food source rather than as an object of popularity. On Macquarie Island where New Zealander Joseph Hatch boiled many thousands of Royal and King penguins for their oil till his license was revoked by popular revulsion, led by the famous Australian explorer, Douglas Mawson. Zoos made the penguins popular. There is a law to protect them today. Cruises to see the penguins have become very popular. On the two cruises I've been on there are passengers from all over the world.

This is expedition cruising at its most demanding and exciting. The winds of Antarctica blow strongly as there is little in their way. At sea, the open and uninterrupted Southern Ocean offers a corridor for the prevailing "west wind drifts". Closer to the continent and south of 55°, contrary currents cause the "east wind drift". In Polar Regions, the strongest winds are born in the cold air of the icecap, blowing down steep slopes, and accelerating under gravity. These "katabatic" (down flowing) winds reach fearsome speeds, with 120 mph common. Many viewers of film of Antarctica have seen pictures of these katabatic winds and would never choose to be caught in such frigid conditions. Last but not least are the "williwaws" these are sudden violent cold wind blowing down from the mountain passes toward the coast.

In 1911-14 Mawson expedition, the Australians recorded gusts of up to 140 mph breaking their anemometer. These winds arrive with disconcerting suddenness, causing severe wind chill and difficult conditions for small boats that the early explorers sailed. These winds would cease as abruptly as they arrive. That is why so many people question why anyone would want to go to Antarctica. You do realize this is during the middle of the summer months and if you will recall the daily temperatures written in the logs are not that cold. Then too you wear the big heavy parka that they issued us on arrival. Actually with thermal underwear and wool sweaters you actually get very warm and overheated while tramping through the soft snow and carrying heavy camera equipment. Our weather at Cape Washington where the beautiful pictures were shot was good beyond the belief of our expedition staff. Frank Todd, one of our naturalist, said they always hope the weather for these landings will be a 5 and the best to hope for was a 10 but that day at Cape Washington it was a 12. The staff just laughed at me when I told of my love affair with the "Weather God." That night they celebrated with me at the bar and toasted that beautiful day.

To continue this discussion on the winds of the gales following a snow storm they lift the new snow and create blizzards, making the driven snow have the erosive power of sand, penetrating everywhere polishing rock that makes travel difficult or even impossible.

CHAPTER 12

IN THE PACK ICE

Day 8 Wednesday, December 10, 2003

Latitude/Longitude:	65°17S, 172°22'E
Wind:	SW, 6 knots
Air Temperature:	2°C/36°F
Sea Temperature:	0°C/32°F

This morning Grigory, our ice-pilot, was taken up in a helicopter and flew ahead of the ship to scout the best possible course to follow economically through the ice pack.

We were all excited to see our first Adelie penguins. They showed up on the floes, along with crab-eater seals and the Antarctic and Snow Petrels.

This was the day that they briefed us on how the Kapitan Khlebnekov works in the ice and the characteristics of the Russian icebreakers. The ship was built in Helsinki, Norway by the Wartsila Company and launched in 1980. I have seen this shipyard in Helsinki. You may be interested in the following facts: it displaces 15,000 tons and 433 ft=132m he is driven by six massive diesel engines, developing 24,200 h.p. These drive six AC generators that power three DC motors, which turn the three 72 ft=22 m long propeller shafts. Cruising speed is 16.5 knots in calm open water; first-year ice 5 ft-1.5 m thick may be broken continuously at 1 kn; 10 ft-3 m thick ice is tackled by repeated ramming. Operating range is 10,500 nautical miles at cruising speed. My hope is that you women readers are interested in these facts because it becomes very important when you are at sea and things are happening.

At 1743 we gathered on the foredeck to drink hot chocolate laced with rum and wait for the magic moment when we crossed over the Antarctic Circle—66°33'. The Longitude was 173°57.2215'E. We celebrated that night

with the Captain's Welcome Cocktail Party, where we met the Bridge and
Engine Room officers formally; we had been meeting often enough causally
over the last few days. After the Captain's Welcome Dinner, we were treated
to a colorful sunset that sent us all running for our cameras.

Remember we are in 24-hour daylight. During my cruises to Antarctica
and the Arctic I have taken fantastic pictures of this kind of light on ice and
snow. The ice appears golden or silver depending on the time of so called
night. This was a good day and night and we all looked forward to a good
nights sleep now that we were in the sea of ice.

CHAPTER 13

WORKING SOUTH IN THE PACK ICE
Day 9 Thursday, December 11, 2003

Latitude/Longitude:	69°12' S, 175°13' E
Wind:	SE, 11 knots
Air Temperature:	3°C/27°F
Sea Temperature:	0°C/32°F

At first we were making good time in very easy sea conditions—open pack with big leads, little wind, and excellent visibility. At 0900, we entered 9/10 packs, and Grigory went up in the helicopter for an ice reconnaissance to find the most practical course ahead. In fact he found the conditions ahead looked pretty much the same with 7-9/10 packs. These reconnaissances always made us feel confident in the care they were taking for our safety.

Susan, our leader, organized the first of our flight seeing trips, giving us a chance to see the ship from up above, offering spectacular photographic opportunities. You can understand why there are so many professional photographers on board. These are opportunities of a lifetime to film these beautiful scenes. From above we saw many Minke whales.

At 1700, we were in the lecture theatre to hear Frank Todd introduce us to Antarctica's most famous denizens—the penguins. Remember Frank is responsible for the exhibit of penguins made famous at Sea World in San Diego. With a sequence of outstanding photographs, he led us through the basics of penguin biology, using three long-tailed or brush-tailed species— Chinstrap, Gentoo and Adelie penguins. We were indeed fortunate to have him with us on this trip—probably the most experienced penguin scientist any of us are ever likely to meet.

The Adelies, which are adorable because they are tiny, very busy little penguins; they seem to race around all over the place. The Adelies are the most abundant of all penguins, the colonies involving many thousands of pairs and the total population being somewhere in the region of two and a half million pairs, half of them here in the Ross Sea area. They are vulnerable to disturbance from scientist and tourists. Our leaders are very strict about our disturbing their habitat. My first expedition we were told not to walk through or into the rookeries. We would have to stay on board if we did so.

When it comes to mating the male will walk 60 miles to reach their breeding grounds. I wrote earlier that most penguins' mate for life but the Adelies due to the harsh climate they live in do not mate for life. After the male goes those 60 miles he will not always wait for last years mate and will bond quickly with an available female. Courtship is brief, with much flapping and guttural gossip. This mating was taking place while we were at their rookery and it was unbelievable the noises they were making. They make their nests with stones that they go to great lengths to find and often steal from other nests. The pebble market becomes a scene of neighborhood theft; bickering (this was part of the sounds I heard) and home improvement, as pebbles move from nest to nest amid jealous parents who skillfully steal from each other but decry the injustice when it happens to them. (There's an old video from my first trip of the gentoos who do the same theft of nests and it entertains everyone who watches it.) They lay two eggs. The incubation is short as 30 days or as long as 43 days, it depends on local conditions. There were no chicks at this time because they hatch in late December, fledge in 50 to 56 days and go to sea in mid-February. The adult Adelie's main diet at this stage is krill that is small enough for them to eat. These krill swarm near the shore at this time of year. The Adelies are born followers. They hang together. They were named by Jules demont Jeurdene after his wife Adelie. Adelies worst enemy is the adverse weather conditions. Snow falling on downy chicks may melt and cause death from chilling. Long-term global warming may be responsible for the current population decline. Now we know that the B15A had blocked their route to sea and was making it impossible to have any food left for their chicks after traveling 60 miles. The chicks did not survive that year.

We made good time all day, averaging 12 knots. By early evening we reached Cape Adare. In a calm sea and zero wind we anchored at Robert's Bay, landing by zodiac on the north beach, just under the Cape at 2330. We had nearly three full hours ashore. We had plenty of time to enjoy a very large Adelie colony, approximately a quarter of a million pair. This was going to be my first filming of penguins and I had to set up my tripod among the rocks, which was difficult.

Because of the cold I had to wear my heavy gloves. These were the new gloves where the fingers were exposed so you can hit the tiny buttons on the camera. This is a subject I would like to discuss with camera manufacturers and that is those small buttons. The camera was left running after it was supposedly turned off because of these buttons. Also I brought the chemical pads that warm the palm of your hands.

On the hike to the rookery the path that our expedition staff had marked for us I slipped and fell backwards. Needless to say I was a bit shaken but not hurt because of my heavy clothes I was well padded. While lying there I held tightly onto my camera to make sure it was not damaged. I then realized there was no one there to help me up. That was the first time I was reminded that I was alone and it was sad time for me. My husband had always been there to pick me up. You must realize that this group of passengers were there to film and they were very independent of one another. So, Gals, you pick yourself up and carry on . . .

CHAPTER 14

THE ROSS SEA—APPROACHING CAPE HALLET
Day 10 Friday, December 12, 2003

Latitude/Longitude:	71°48'S, 171°53'E
Wind:	NE, 11 knots
Air Temperature:	6°C/43°F
Sea Temperature:	0°C/32°F

We were in the Ross Sea, and it was another fine day. We were on our way to Cape Hallet, and enjoying great weather. All morning we sailed through pristine, first-year pack, with the Admiralty Mountains, in all their snow-covered glory, on our starboard.

We had a briefing session at 1115 that prepared us for an early lunch and a helicopter landing on the fast-ice by a grounded iceberg. We walked over the snow and very carefully avoiding treacherously slippery sections, to the stony plain under a picturesque cape. The expedition leaders always go and scout the terrain and mark the path with red flags. These areas are notorious for crevasses and they made sure we were safe. This level plateau was home to many thousands of Adelies, again most of them incubating their clutch of two eggs on their stony nests.

Everyone was back on board at 1815. With recap delayed to 1900. (Everyday we would have a recap of the day's adventure). We would also learn what plans Susan would have for us tomorrow. Now that it was smooth sailing we also liked to have a day where we could catch up with sleep, log writing, camera cleaning and digital filing. I also had my bridge games to play.

ADLIE PENGUINS

CAPE HALLET

CHAPTER 15

THE ROSS SEA TOWARDS CAPE WASHINGTON

Day 11 Saturday, December 13, 2003

Latitude/Longitude:	74°27'S, 168°59'E
Wind:	NE, 8 knots
Air Temperature:	2°C/28°F
Sea Temperature:	0°C/32°F

This was an overcast morning with a spectacular view of Mount Melbourne rising in a snowy glow. We were steaming through first-year pack, mostly 7/10, film of emergent ice—grease ice—on the surface of the water. As the day wore on the ice became serious, averaging 9 and even 10/10, with many pressures ridges, so that by that afternoon, we were down to slow speed, often with five of the six engines running.

At times this great ship was forced to a standstill, having to back off far enough to stop and go ahead again, gathering speed to ram into the barrier and gain a few more feet. I took some excellent moving pictures of this action. Everyone who sees these pictures is amazed as the ship rams upon the ice until it makes a crack and then it backs up and proceeds to follow these cracks. You have to see it to believe it is happening. However, it is slow going and in our wake were huge blocks of ice torn from our path; many turned over and showed the ochre-brown algae clinging underneath. It is a great source of food for zooplankton, fish and Snow Petrels.

MT. ERBUS

CAPE WASHINGTON

Our next target was Cape Washington where we would see the Emperor Penguins. With our current speed it was going to be a while before we were able to helicopter to the rookery. Our penguin specialist, Frank gave us a lecture about these emperors. I could not believe we were this close to them. This was the cruise chosen just to see and film these Lords of Antarctica and it was so exciting to know that we had arrived.

We finally reached a docking position in the fast ice. They call this garaging. After an early dinner, John and Steve, our helicopter pilots fired up the helicopters and we were shuttled ashore to land on the fast ice behind stranded icebergs, shielded from the view of a large gathering of emperors. At last, and in wonderful evening light we were able to trudge through a half-mile of snow and come close to these superb birds. Most of the adults were at sea fishing, but some were still standing about and feeding their young ones. The sound of the penguins especially the chicks begging for more food I call a symphony. This is a penguin symphony because no two families have the same call. This makes a harmony of their sounds. However, I did learn to distinguish the male from the female calls.

There was a continual stream of adults tobogganing their way across the fast ice, coming or going to feed their chicks or to leave the colony for a fishing trip. Remember these chicks are born in the middle of the Antarctic winter—June—and they have to obtain their full growth by December so that they then go to sea to feed and become adult penguins. They do not return to this rookery for years.

Of all the penguin species these are the first ones I saw that were tobogganing on their bellies. The emperors grow up to 4 feet tall. The males have to put on at least 30 pounds of fat to maintain them while they hatch the egg. The emperors toboggan because their weight is too much for their very short legs. These legs are short because they are not kept warm by feathers. The extreme winter cold makes it necessary to have as little exposure as possible. So they handle this extra weight by flopping down on their bellies and using their flippers as the force that pushes them. Their wings are extended but not very useful in this tobogganing. I loved to watch them travel across the snow. This also keeps their bellies so clean that my pictures show them shining like silver in this beautiful sunshine. I filmed from 1900 to 0100 on this outing. The low sunlight on the snow was perfect for filming. Once we arrived at the rookery I set up my tripod and filmed constantly. I only moved my position once.

I must tell you how the penguins regarded us. You see they have never seen a human being especially one dressed in a bright red parka and bright yellow slickers. I have some wonderful shoots of four chicks who were led by the biggest one—I called him "Empy"—that were checking me out. I was filming on a mound and they came up to it cautiously and got as close as they dare. I did not move a muscle so they wouldn't be scared away. Now all the time they are chattering. They decided that they did not know what it was and as they waddled away they were saying—"I don't know what it is." Another thing about these chicks when they are frightened they flap their wings—and their wings were really flapping.

While on the subject of the chick's behavior they were also frightened by the noise of the helicopters flying overhead. I took many shots of them flapping their wings showing how frightened they were of this noise. I really felt we had invaded their territory. Poor babies!! I must say though that the adults never showed any notice of this helicopter noise—just the chicks.

I filmed for five hours and headed back to catch the last helicopter to the ship. This trek through the snow that was soft was one that will not be forgotten. There are times when I am reminded of my age and this was one of them. My camera equipment was heavy. I was overdressed. Whenever you go on these excursions you dress for the cold. That day I was overdressed and the exertion really overheated me. When people ask me how you tolerated the cold I am reminded of those times when the activity overheated me. We all had the same problem with overdressing but the winds can come up at a moments notice and you need the warmth. This is a minor discomfort when you look around you and see that pristine beauty. You feel like you are invading some ones privacy in these surroundings.

Try to picture the beautiful icebergs that have been locked into this frozen sea. Most of them show that they have rolled over and that's why they are beautifully sculpted. There is one shot of an iceberg that is black and with the sunshine on it looks silver. This black is caused by the volcanic eruption of Mount Erbus that can be seen in the background. I was surrounded by beautiful scenery.

When we got back to the ship we saw a pod of killer whales. They were swimming between the fast ice and the drifting pack. The ship had made an opening in the ice where they could capture the penguins while they were feeding and have there own feast.

CHAPTER 16

CAPE WASHINGTON

Day 12 Sunday, December 14, 2003

Latitude/Longitude:	74°40'S, 165°27'E
Wind:	NW, 13 knots
Air Temperature:	2°C/36°F
Sea Temperature:	0°C/32°F

We spent the night at our ice-dock or as they called "garaging" the ship. Some people stayed out all night filming the penguins. The ship remained secure, with a gangway leading down invitingly to the ice. Penguins were taking advantage of the lead opened by the Kapitan Khlebnikov, and were leaping out of the sea just behind the ship, then setting off in a one mile line over the ice towards the rookery. There is another observation I made about the Emperor Penguins that they were so disciplined about their travels back and forth to the rookeries. It's called their highways and they always just followed the penguin ahead of them—no crowding in line. I wish we humans could be so well behaved.

At 1250 our fine ship backed off, turned and sailed south. That afternoon we sailed the open water off the Drygalski Tongue where there were miles and miles of the sculptured ice-cliffs. These are unbelievably beautiful. Again I was reminded that this is another world on this planet called earth. The ship is crunching through multi-year ice as we enter an ice canyon. They decide to dock here overnight and garage the ship into the ice. With the gangway down and safe areas with our marked flags, we were able to hike through the icy canyon. In the distance there were ice-cliffs both to the right and left of us. We also had a visit from Weddell seals that were loafing around a seal-hole in the ice. Many of them obliged us by posing and scratching their heads and assuming indolent postures.

We were treated to a special occasion by being carried by a helicopter onto the top of an ice shelf where the crew had set up an ice bar with bottles of champagne. It was such fun to be drinking champagne and looking out from the top of this ice shelf. Much to my embarrassment while walking away from the helicopter I went up to my knees in the snow and proceeded to fall down and got up laughing as one of the men ran to my rescue. Then I got into discussions as to why I have been falling and I was told to glide over the snow. Fortunately, the snow was soft.

This was the night that we were told if we so choose we could sleep out on the ice. They provided survival tents (some of the passengers had actually brought their own sleeping bags) and sleeping bags. It was interesting that 15 of the women chose to sleep out on the ice but none of the men. I was recovering from a virus that was being circulated among the passengers and I felt it would not be wise to sleep on the ice. I was sorry because it makes for a great story. So you see you do not freeze to death in Antarctica . . .

CHAMPAGNE ON TOP OF A GLACIER

CAPE WASHINGTON

CHAPTER 17

DRYGALSKI ICE TONGUE/B15A ICEBERG

Day 13 Monday, December 15, 2003

Latitude/Longitude:	75°27'S, 165°30'E
Wind:	N, 8 knots
Air Temperature:	1°C/36°F
Sea Temperature:	0°C/32°F

We had great weather while we docked in the fast ice canyon off the Drygalski Ice Tongue. We took advantage of this good weather and at 0930 Tim and Lorne set off across the ice towards the sculptured cliffs. They looked close. They announced a trek through this area. For an hour they trudged (this is why I didn't go). I don't like to trudge in those soft snowy conditions. I could enjoy looking at these cliffs from the ship.

Later in the morning our highly appreciated galley staff had set up a barbecue out in the open on the foredeck in brilliant sunshine as the ship slowly sailed back out and headed north.

This was our furthest south position of 75°27.9294'S, 165°30.5508'E. I hope all you sailors who read this appreciate detailed positioning of the ship. That is what is great about expedition cruising these facts become important. Now when I am looking at a map I know exactly where we were sailing.

Threading our way through dense three feet to six feet fast ice we were guided by Grigory, the ice pilot, flying ahead of us in the helicopter. The afternoon was characterized by beautiful ice scenery, till the sun gave in and the clouds took over. Heavier ice meant that the Captain ordered a fourth engine to be fired up. At recap, Susan spoke of the massive tabular iceberg, named B15A, which had broken off the Ross Ice Shelf. Drifting from its birthplace in the Bay of Whales (Amundsen may well have sledged across this very piece) the iceberg found temporary grounding on this west side of the Ross Sea. We saw it that evening on our way to Coulman Island. Tony reminded everyone that underneath the desert of ice we were sailing through, there were fish, especially adapted to deal with the near-zero temperatures.

Tim's girlfriend was on board and she was a scuba diver who loved to go below the ice. Of course she was a Nordic—I am not sure whether she was from Sweden or Norway but I do remember she was a beautiful blond. I had been on a dive boat cruise in the British Virgin Islands and when I discussed this with her she said that the icy cold seas were where she preferred to dive. She did assure me that the equipment today does protect the diver from the cold as long as you do not stay down too long. I still prefer snorkeling in the warm Caribbean and its beauty.

An interesting fact about the Antarctic fish is that they have adapted to the near freezing water. One species the Trematomus Bernacchi actually lives under fast-ice because they have lipoproteins—antifreeze proteins—in the blood and body tissues. The ice fish are one large and predatory group and are unique in having no red blood cells. Lacking the oxygen carried by hemoglobin and myoglobin, they manage because the Antarctic water is well oxygenated. The clear blood and pale anemic flesh of these fish give them their family name even the gills are cream colored, in contrast to the red gills of most fish.

At this recap we have a very special exhibit by Frank, our penguin expert; this is when he showed us the abandon emperor egg that he had collected earlier. He told us of his breeding success at Sea World and the mortality among the penguins of this region. If you want to learn more about penguins Frank is your "man."

In this briefing Susan told us we would see the great tabular iceberg B15A. It is said to be 170 by 35 KM (icebergs are measured in kilometers). It is 100 miles long and 98 feet high and 20 miles wide. After dinner it was already in sight. From about 2130, the Kapitan Khlebnikov was edging closer to the massive tabular, which stretched as far as we could see into the distance. A lot of people watched from the comfort and warmth of the bridge but I choose to watch from the flying bridge. The foredeck was crowded with berg-watchers. Still the sun shone and there was mercifully little wind. Yes, it was cold but tolerable. Again our Quark parkas (which we came to call our "Quarkas") gave us the warmth we needed. I repeat when you dress properly the cold is not a problem.

It was exciting as Susan called over the PA system that we were one mile off, then a half mile, then slowly but inexorably the ship closed the face of the berg; till it towered 98 feet above us, ever so slowly we closed the distance, till we almost touched the face of the icy cliff. For a moment the ship held off, then at 2235, we with the merest touch ahead, the mighty icebreaker eased forward and the stemhead crunched into the ice. We were at 75°57.2'S 168°50.7'E. A barrow load of ice tumbled onto the deck, many thousand of years in the making. Tim and Rod attacked the ice with ice axes to reduce them to manageable size. From ancient snowfall feeding the icy desert of the continental mass and by way of the Beardmore Glacier and a meeting with the sea at the Bay of Whales far to our east, B15A provided Elke, our bartender with the most exclusive pure ice for the bar. In no time it was introduced to whisky and celebratory drinks all around, providing a rousing end to the day. I had my usual cuba-libra drink with this ice and truly believe it did taste better because of the beautiful clear thousands of years old ice. Actually I broke my rule of one drink and had another cuba-libra. This is what memories are made of . . . still the sun shone as we turned in for the night knowing we were sailing for another penguin island.

I would like to tell you about the "Rogue' tabulars. They are large calvings, with a linear dimension of more than 12 mile from the Great Antarctic ice shelves of the Ross and Weddell seas, amongst others, are classified according to their origins and history. I hope you all are aware of this calving that is causing the water levels to rise in our oceans. I have also seen the glaciers calving in Alaska. They make loud sounds like a canon going off. I was living dangerously in Alaska when they would take our zodiacs right up to the face of the glaciers. Thank goodness we were far enough away from some of the calving that took place when we went up to glaciers in zodiacs.

Sorry, back to Antarctica. To identify the icebergs they go from sector 0° to 90°W (which includes the Filchner Ice Shelf in the Weddell Sea) are given the prefix A, while those from the quadrant 90° to 180°W (including the Ross Sea) begin with a B. This is followed by a figure that defines the position in the calving sequence, and a letter defining the timing of the break from the parent iceberg, B15 was the longest iceberg, at 305 linear km190 ft ever observed. The segment B15A was the one we "kissed." The segment B15J was the most recent calving from its parent. Do note that they write of these icebergs as families. This comes from those who work with these facts feeling a real attachment to their working knowledge.

B15A and its children are still causing real problems for shipping and the penguin colonies in the Ross Sea. This has made the news as of December 29, 2004 the world became aware of this very iceberg. All those wonderful little Adelie penguin's lives were threatened because their highway to the sea is now blocked and their food source is cut off. Also the research facilities no longer have a waterway to bring in their supplies. This is happening in the very area that we were sailing. It is very strange to be so far away from this tragedy and yet feel so close to the whole scene. I have been very aware of the ice of Antarctica melting and have I kept abreast of all the news since my first trip to the Antarctica Peninsula in 1992. This makes the news very real to me and my concern is very serious.

B15A ICEBERG

CHAPTER 18

APPROACHING COULMAN ISLAND

Day 14 Tuesday, December 16, 2003

Latitude/Longitude:	73°44' S, 170°42' E
Wind:	Variable, 4 knots
Air Temperature:	30°C/37°F
Sea Temperature:	0°C/32°F

Early morning found us sailing an open, flat calm sea, this is one of the fascinating experiences of sailing in Antarctica. You never can be prepared for what the new day will bring. The pack had increased and slowed us down as we approached Coulman Island. We reached the fast ice in Lady Newnes Bay off the northwest of the island at 1100 and after several ramming maneuvers, the Kapitan Khlebnikov was safely garaged in this ice-dock by 1145, and Susan had organized an early lunch so we were free to go out on the ice.

There were emperor penguins to the left of us, and in front of us, so there was no need for the helicopters to take us to them. Penguins thronged over the ice. We were close to the water's edge so we had a grandstand view of the activity of the rookery. Many adults were tobogganing to and from the congregation of their chicks. These chicks will soon be joining them and going to sea. Chicks cannot toboggan because their fuzzy feathery bodies are not smooth enough. The adult penguins tobogganed along their highways. They would curve around on the ice field. It was as disciplined as was mentioned before but so characteristic of penguin behavior.

This highway was almost a half-mile ahead of the ship. Tim and Rod flagged a route to give us a complete tour of the colony. There was plenty of activity with strings of fat emperors making their way past us. Also we were able to see a marauding leopard seal. There was the sad experience of seeing the digital sequences of a leopard seal leap onto the ice and grab a fat emperor. I was so glad that I did not personally witness this happening to an emperor penguin because I want to protect them from harm. I won't forget the look on that penguin's face as it was dragged away. Believe me I also have strong feelings about man's inhumanity to man.

Photographer's light was the order of the day. This light provided me with such beautiful shots. My Sony DV300 Handycam took beautiful pictures of Antarctica. It is going to make a good film.

The film shot today was a gift from a group of young adult male penguins. These are young because I learned to tell the age of the penguins by how bright the orange coloring is on their necks. Also I determined that this was a gang of males from their calls and they had probably gone to sea as chicks and were hanging out together. They have to be five years old before they breed. They have not yet found a mate.

They were going to be very close. (We are not permitted to get within 50 yards of the penguins) so instead of folding up my tripod I set it up just in time to start filming. They were so close that I could not change camera lens. I still remember how exciting it was when they stopped right in front of me. It was too close to get full body shots. They proceeded to preen themselves and rid their bodies of the parasites that they attract from the sea. They hung out for a while then turned and started tobogganing back to the sea. A couple of them looked right into my camera as if to say: "take my picture." Unlike the chicks who were afraid of me these boys just looked at me. I shot these emperors tobogganing away from me on their way back to sea. It is one of my favorite scenes.

The last stragglers came back along the snowy path and over the sastrugi and were all aboard by 1900. The Kaptian Khlebnikov extricated himself (please remember, icebreakers are 'he') from the garage, backing and filling to maneuver through a field of heavy pack, which had inconveniently been tide-borne to hem us in during the afternoon. For a person such as me this was an impressive sight of ship handling—Russian seamen sure know their ice. It took one and three-quarters of an hour to turn the ship around to face seaward, only to be looking at a heavy field of tide-driven pack. At 2130 the Captain decided to sit it out and wait for a tide change and for the currents to clear the pack away.

CHAPTER 19

At Sea

Day 15 Wednesday, December 17, 2003

Latitude/Longitude:	73°02'S, 171°24'E
Wind:	Variable, 8 knots
Air Temperature:	1°C/30°F
Sea Temperature:	0°C/32°F

At 0430, the tides did their work and by 0515, the Kapitan Khlebnikov was free and into open water, heading north towards Possession Island. It was overcast and cold morning, a good time to go to the lecture theatre for two excellent talks, first by Lorne, looking back to tell the Borchgrevink story, and then by Tim, who unraveled the mystery of sea ice in all its manifestations.

Ross seals were seen this morning. It should be noted that this species, which is confined to pack ice, is commonly noted in the literature as being "rare and little known." It was rarely recorded until recently, but the advent of the Russian icebreakers traveling with Quark Expeditions has added a great deal of knowledge about its distribution and behavior. The Ross Seal was the last discovered and is the least known of all pinnipeds. Captain James Clark Ross found them at 68°S 176°E and collected two specimens during the British Antarctic Expedition of 1839-43, aboard HMS Erebus and HMS Terror. Naming a ship Terror sure tells it like it is!!!

We reached Cape Roget, on the Borchgrevink coast, just south of Possession, at 1330, but a scout helicopter party found that conditions were unsuitable for a landing. The fast ice was clearly breaking up, which meant that it was unadvisable for the icebreaker to accelerate the process by ramming the edge to make a dock, with the danger of sending emperor juveniles to sea before they were ready. Also, there had been a recent snowfall, which meant that the helicopters could not land, because swirling snow whipped up by the rotors would create impossible visibility. So, in the hope that conditions might change Susan decided to make for Possession Island.

By 1430 we were approaching the Possession group, though visibility was not great. Clouds of Antarctic Petrels greeted us as we closed the main island, which was the scene of James Clark Ross's landing on January 12, 1840, when he hoisted the Union flag and claimed 500 miles of new coastline for the Crown, naming it Victoria Land, in honor of his Queen.

We did not go ashore here at Possession Island because of weather conditions. This was a great disappointment to us. This cruise was taken to see as many penguins as possible and we needed more pictures but weather dictates when we can go ashore. Susan called us all on the foredeck for groups photograph with Ross's landing place clearly visible in the background. Then the Kapitan Khlebnikov sailed on, the wind picked up, it became colder, visibility got worse, and we were reminded that life here in the Antarctic is not all sunshine and glassy calms. This again made me so thankful for the beautiful night of filming the emperors at Cape Washington. I think this might be a good place to quote Apsley Cherry-Gerrard (Member of Scott's 1910-13 Expedition) "An Antarctic expedition is the worst way to have the best time of your life." I heartily agree because it is an experience that is never forgotten and I would do again.

Wouldn't you like to know the curious history of those penguins which had been ill advisedly introduced to the Northern Hemisphere? Penguins cannot tolerate warm seawater. The extreme limit of their range is marked by a line linking places with a mean annual air temperature of 20°C/68°F (surface waters are warmed accordingly) so they are effectively trapped by a thermal barrier and restricted to the cold waters of the Southern Hemisphere. An ill-fated experiment introduced a small number of Kings, Macaroni and Jackass (Gentoos) Penguins to the Lofoten Islands off the Norwegian coast in 1936-38. The last recorded sighting was in 1954. Some suffered at the hands of the local people who regarded them as bogeymen. None attempted to nest, probably because there weren't enough of them to encourage the noisy sociability that stimulates courtship. (Penguins breed freely enough in northern zoos, when they are kept in good numbers in close proximity.) But the experiment was not a good idea anyway. Auks occupy the equivalent niche in northern latitudes and are a hugely successful family, not needing competition from alien penguins. They are not related to penguins but look alike, because they are designed for the same way of life. This is a classic example of convergent evolution. I saw these Auks when I was in the Arctic and never in my mind compared them to the penguins.

CHAPTER 20

THE ROSS SEA

Day 16 Thursday, December 18, 2003

Latitude/longitude:	71°21'S, 172°12'E
Wind:	SSE, 45 knots
Air Temperature:	3°C/27°F
Sea Temperature:	0°C/32°F

Through the night conditions slowly became less favorable: the wind picked up to gale force 8, then 9, approaching storm force 10. Visibility remained poor, with blizzards. This was not a night for sleeping. Now having told you earlier that my bunk is the "rocking chair" which meant that these heavy seas during the night would have me sliding unto the corner table if I didn't grab onto the handle at the head of my bunk. Now when we were in heavy seas we were told to secure our cabins. That means luggage and everything on the desk and shelves must be secured. I made sure that all my bathroom articles were tucked away. You leave nothing to chance with these warnings. Now my roommate had taken enough of her seasick pills and the railing was up on her bunk that she slept through one of the roughest seas I have ever encountered. I was confident that this ship was built for these waves and the only time I became frightened is when the engines stopped. Now that was because the props were out of the water for just a second that seemed a lot longer to me. I had visions of being tossed about in this raging sea without an engine. But it quickly came back on and we battled those waves like a true icebreaker. I still feel a tingle when this moment is recalled. These storms are the reason that do I not like to be on the upper decks. Some of those passengers on the 8th deck were thrown out of their bunks. Now this is not to discourage you from this adventure because you have to realize just where you are sailing.

Oh, yes, I must mention how cool and calm the servers are when we have to eat in this kind of motion. They pour water on all the linen tablecloths so our dishes won't slide about which did not always work. We really didn't need water or liquids at this time. But we did eat—those who were not seasick. Another thing I must mention again that the doctor on board had special seasick pills for those in need.

The next morning visibility remained poor, with blizzards. So Susan and the Captain decided there was no longer any chance of a further continental landing. The Kaptian Khlebnikov headed north. We had been lucky to see the coast and the penguins in exceptionally good conditions. With the gale winds behind us, the ship had as easy motion and made for the extra comfort of the pack. Soon after breakfast we were sailing through open pack and more-or-less sea. You really appreciate even a more-or-less calm sea after our rough ride through the storm we had just encountered.

With the wind continuing to howl they filled our day with lectures and videos.

CHAPTER 21

NORTH BOUND—RECROSSING THE ANTARCTIC CIRCLE

Day 17 Friday, December 19, 2003

Latitude/Longitude:	67°33'S, 175°45'E
Wind:	SE, 21 knots
Air Temperature:	1°C/30°F
Sea Temperature:	0°C/32°F

While the winds were still strong, the ship was working a reasonably calm sea as we were in pack varying between 3 and 9/10. Visibility was still poor, so there was no chance of reconnaissance flights in the helicopter for Gregory, and we simply held a compass course instead of chasing leads. It is really much more interesting to chase leads. The assumption was that we would be in varying degrees of pack till we re-entered the Southern Ocean. At approximately 61°S we crossed the Antarctic Circle and headed north. Weather charts revealed that we were in the eye of bad weather, conditions being more favorable both to the north and south.

Susan organized another day of lectures and events. Frank spoke of Antarctic seals and whales. There was an engine tour that I had taken on my Arctic cruise.

Remember, I mentioned we had Lisa Trotter our scuba diver who preferred diving under the ice. Well, she showed us riveting video footage taken by her underwater cameras, revealing the colorful life of invertebrates and benthic plants in the shallow waters of the Antarctic Peninsula.

Tim and Loren Dolman encouraged everyone to submit images for a grand photo presentation planned for the end of the trip. Loren did his best to make us understand the intricacies of Antarctic politics and the Antarctic

Treaty System. These lectures were like listening to National Geography television programs with all the information that was forthcoming. We were all looking forward to the New Zealand Sub-Antarctic islands. Then at 1915 we crossed the Antarctic Circle. There were always announcements made whenever we crossed the lines.

CHAPTER 22

AT SEA—LEAVING THE PACK ICE

Day 18 Saturday, December 20, 2003

Latitude/Longitude:	65°04'S, 170°19'E
Wind:	S, 23 knots
Air Temperature:	2°C/28°F
Sea Temperature:	0°C/32°F

We were running on four engines this morning at breakfast time because we were sailing through heavy 10 by 10 pack ice. Now and then, we went out into open water . . . it was going to be an interesting day. One of the things about expedition cruising is that we can spend time on the bridge observing the seas we are encountering. I spent a lot of time on the bridge. The weather was bright but cloudy, with visibility somewhat improved. At 1030, we passed what was probably our last Emperor Penguin.

Quite a lot of crab-eater seals were seen during the day, lounging on new snow on the pack, and wriggling away if we happened to inadvertently pass too close for their comfort. Snow Petrels and Antarctic Petrels were the birds of the day, as well as a lone Southern Fulmar that kept following us for a few hours.

At teatime, there was the first faint movement of the ocean swells. These days at sea were very relaxing. I was happy to have my bridge buddies. There was always time spent reading and looking at the books in the library. There was quite an enthusiastic group of artists who really enjoyed themselves.

CHAPTER 23

AT SEA NORTH BOUND

Day 19 Sunday, December 21, 2003

Latitude/Longitude:	60°22'S, 169°48'E
Wind:	SE, 31 knots
Air Temperature:	1°C/30°F
Sea Temperature:	0°C/32°F

The overnight swell developed as we entered a moderate sea and entered the open ocean. The Antarctic and Snow Petrels had already been replaced by Cape Petrels—Pintados—and Black-browed Albatrosses appeared again. The bird watchers would spend hours on the deck filming these birds.

By midday, we were enjoying that old-time rock and roll again. We were not permitted to go up to the bridge, flying bridge, foredeck, and after deck were closed to sea watchers.

Tony gave a talk outlining the history of whaling, entitled "That She Blows!" He reminded a skeptical audience that, until recently, whaling was regarded as an honorable trade and whalers with great respect. My respect for the whalers was lost when I visited Shackleton's grave in Grytviken on South Georgia. We walked through a deserted whaling station and saw all the equipment that they used to make whale oil. The thought of the magnificent animals being destroyed like that was horrifying. Man certainly proved that brainpower wins over size. Back to Tony's talk. Fishermen from the Basque region were the earliest—whaling off Newfoundland a thousand years ago—and for a long time they were the most skilled exponents. From the earliest times, they hunted fin whales in the Bay of Biscay—fin tongues were regarded as a great delicacy by the Norman French. Basques were employed by both English and Dutch whaling expeditions working in the waters of

Spitsbergen, in the 17th century. Whale oil had numerous uses, it was much valued, and the companies made enormous profits. When Spitsbergen stock of bowheads were vastly depleted, the whalers penetrated west to the Davis Strait. When those were in turn reduced, they turned their attentions to the South Atlantic, whose rich resources had been discovered by Cook in 1775. However, it was not until the very early days of the 20th century, and by virtue of the invention of the Foyn harpoon gun, that the most devastating destruction of the southern whales began. By the 1930's the stocks were in decline, so the whaling companies agreed to quotas to reduce oil production. Several ineffectual international agreements finally resulted in the Antarctica Treaty of 1959, whose object was to preserve Antarctica as a region of peace and international co-operation. This fragile agreement is working—so far, but it has no role in the control of whaling. Whales are still highly regarded, though less so because of their oil: and the whale fishery is the subject of much heart-searching. I wrote about the whaling station earlier.

Because of my concern about the preservation of Antarctica the following is a copy of Tony's writing about the "The Antarctica Treaty System: Problems and Prospects" The Antarctic Treaty was one of the results of the scientific cooperation during the International Geophysical Year (IGY) of 1957-58. The International Council of Scientific Unions, to coordinate the work of twelve countries with Antarctic stations, had formed a special Committee on Antarctic Research. This functioned very effectively and, largely in consequence, a high degree of cooperation ensued. These instigated diplomatic discussions were able to resolve many of the international tensions about sovereignty over Antarctic regions by the Antarctic Treaty. The same twelve countries that participated in the IGY made the Antarctic Treaty on December 1, 1959. It came into force after all had ratified it, on June 23, 1961. Antarctica, south of 60 degrees South, then became a continent for science and peace. Subsequently, the Scientific Committee on Antarctic Research was formed in 1958: the Agreed Measures for the Conservation of Flora and Fauna were developed in 1964; the Convention for the Conservation of Antarctic Seals in 1972; the Convention of Antarctic Marine Living Resources in 1980; and the Protocol on Environmental Protection to the Antarctic Treaty in 1991—all of which make up the Antarctic Treaty System. The Antarctic Treaty currently has 45 signatory countries covering 88 percent of the Earth's population. The Treaty deals with seven sovereign claims (Argentina, Australia, Britain, Chile, France, New Zealand, and Norway, some of which conflict) and regulates most human activities. Most current military activities in the treaty region are to provide logistic support of stations and for hydrographic survey. Neither nuclear explosions nor disposal of radioactive waste have been reported in the Treaty region.

To tell you how important the treaty is in protecting the seals. My personal experience on my first cruise was on the Peninsula where we went ashore by zodiac to visit a seal colony. Our naturalist advised us to not get too close to the seals. The reason for this is that the seals had imprinted into their memory bank that man is his enemy. The seal at one time trusted man and consequently man took advantage of this fact. Man would walk right up to the seals and club them to death for their furs. I was walking on a path where I came too close to a seal and he in no uncertain terms was going to let me pass him. Our naturalists all carried a club of wood just in case we met with an encounter such as this. We in no way intended to harm the seal but I did have to pass by him. These seals had learned to survive from man. To think the seal has passed this knowledge down through the genes is amazing.

CHAPTER 24

AT SEA—TOWARDS CAMPBELL ISLAND

Day 20 Monday, December 22, 2003

Latitude/Longitude:	54°51'S 169°27'E
Wind:	SE, 27 knots
Air Temperature:	4°C/39°F
Sea Temperature:	7°C/45°F

During the night we re-crossed the Antarctic Convergence, leaving the biological Antarctic behind us. Due to the rough seas and weather we were saddened by the fact that we did not see all the species of penguins that are only found in this area. I hoped to film the Yellow-eyed Penguins and the Macaronis but the Weather God again showed his dominance and reminded me that I'm just a lowly human being at his mercy. And mercy it was as the seas had really demanded my respect on this cruise. Tourism numbers have doubled since 1950. Tony Soper calls it "TOURISM ON ICE." There are opportunities and constraints of Antarctic Tourism. The Antarctic and the subantarctic have the most magnificent and largely uninhabited wilderness area on Earth.

Many expedition travelers like me seek this beautiful wilderness. Living here in Newport Beach you really find the contrast in the environment a wonderful experience. The beauty and those wonderful funny waddling penguins made me feel so alive.

Extensive mountain chains, glaciers, icebergs, pack ice, and abundant wildlife characterize the Antarctic region. When compared to my expedition cruises to the Arctic and Alaska this area is more pristine. Of course, remember that the Eskimos and the Inuits can live in the northern Arctic where only the researchers can survive in Antarctic in such dire conditions. I was so glad that my cruises to Alaska and the Arctic were before Antarctica. North Pole is beautiful but the remoteness, inaccessibility, and severe climate made Antarctica more of a challenge.

The new static's on tourism in Antarctica have doubled in 2002-2003. Six years ago 6000 tourist visited Antarctica and when I went in 2003 it was 13,571 tourists. Both of the ships that I have cruised on were built for the ice. However, the new ship in 1992 was built with a strengthened ice hull. It could not have made the cruise to the Ross Sea. The only true tourist icebreakers are the two Quark Russian ships.

The majority of tourists originate from the USA, Germany, Britain, and Australia. Only five percent of the tourists visit the Ross Sea region. Felt it was such a privilege to be one of these tourists.

The following is copied from Tony's log: The 1991 Protocol on Environmental Protection to the Antarctic Treaty regulates human activities in Antarctica. Under the Protocol, tourists' operators must conduct an environmental impact assessment of their activities in order to identify and reduce impacts of tourism on the environment. In 1994, the Antarctic Treaty countries adopted recommendations on tourism and non-governmental activities. Recommendation XVII-1 (Guidance for Visitors to the Antarctic) concerns the protection of wildlife and protected areas, respecting scientific research, safety, and impact on the environment. The International Association of Antarctica Tour Operators (IAATO) has adopted these measures and advocates the practice of safe and environmentally responsible private-sector travel to the Antarctic.

CHAPTER 25

AT ANCHOR IN PERSEVERANCE HARBOR, CAMPBELL ISLAND

Day 21 Tuesday, December 23, 2003

Latitude/Longitude:	52°32'S, 169°09'E
Wind:	E, 14 knots
Air Temperature:	6°C/43°F
Sea Temperature:	8°C/46°F

We made a stop at Campbell Island. This is specifically to see and film the nesting albatrosses. The albatrosses are legendary birds, partly because of their great size, but also because they inhabit such remote and storm-ridden seas.

Early 17th century mariners respected their grace and majesty in flight and generally disapproved of killing them at a time when most birds were valued as food. They also believed that the souls of drowned sailors were reincarnated in albatrosses, increasing the fear that killing them would bring bad luck. I wrote earlier how all that changed when they killed them to make pouches, rugs and pipe stems. Now it is the fishermen who are catching them in their nets. Albatrosses are the only bird that can fly around the world. When I first saw the albatross in Antarctic we were told that they would go great distances without food and to preserve their strength they would glide with that magnificent 8-ft wingspan. The air currents supply their ability to glide. They said you would never see an albatross flap its wings because they need to conserve their energy for long flights. To experience there beauty on my first voyage to Antarctic I went out on the bow of the ship and joined another passenger watching the albatross. I'm one of those people who like to communicate with animals so I waved my arms and much to my surprise it flapped its wings. My husband questioned this fact but I had another passenger as a witness. I felt honored by this beautiful bird.

Campbell Island is the most southerly of the New Zealand sub Antarctic islands. We had Marj Wright on board for the whole cruise and her sole purpose was to represent the New Zealand government's environmental protection. We became totally aware of her responsibilities when we entered the New Zealand territories. On the one mile hike we made to the nesting Royal Albatrosses we had to walk on a boardwalk built on the path so that none of the natural environment would be damaged in any way by our footsteps. Now you have to picture our group with backpacks and cameras passing one another on a foot-wide raised wood plank path. Yes, we faced each other as we carefully passed one another. Didn't mind their efforts of preservation but they could have made it wide enough for two people. It was really a disappointing trek because we were told it was the largest of the rookeries. I mentioned earlier that I had seen hundreds of albatrosses in the Falklands that were nesting on the cliffs with their newborn chicks. It was a grueling hike up to the nests and I only got four pictures of the albatrosses. However, the New Zealand government in addition to the boardwalk built a platform for taking pictures. They are really serious about conservation.

After dinner that night we enjoyed a splendid show of assorted digital pictures and movies taken by a dozen of the passengers. All the pictures were of high quality and outstandingly beautiful. Remember, we had all those professional photographers aboard. They ask me to show mine but I declined because I needed to edit the pictures. Previously many of the passengers would sit with me while playing my disks, so they had seen my pictures. I hope those who view my movie will appreciate my being there in the Ross Sea in Antarctica with the Emperor Penguins and all the surrounding beauty.

CHAPTER 26

THE AUCKLAND ISLANDS

Day 22 Wednesday, December 24, 2003, Christmas Eve

Latitude/Longitude:	50°49'S, 166°29'E
Wind:	E, 25 knots
Air Temperature:	8°C/46°F
Sea Temperature:	10°C/50°F

We endured heavy seas overnight, meaning fitful sleep for most. But again I love the rolling of the ship and slept well. When we approached Enderby Island's Sandy Bay there was a healthy swell making conditions clearly unsuitable for a landing when we saw the waves pounding on the beach. We did not go ashore on the zodiacs and much to my regret did not see the yellow-eyed penguins.

This was Christmas Eve and our dinner menu that night was a typical English menu. The English have their Christmas dinner on the eve of Christmas.

We then retired to the lounge to sing Christmas Carols. What fun it was to have Silent Night sung in three languages. I had never heard it in sung in Taiwanese. Tim and Lisa were our Christmas penguins. They dressed as Adelies and were a delight. Rod was our jolly Santa Claus with a flowing white beard and the red Santa Claus suit and he entered bearing a bag of Christmas gifts. (I must tell you that these gifts were contributions from the passengers of things that we brought but did not use. We gift wrapped them and it was fun to see what the passengers got as a gift.) Can you believe I received my own contribution—what are the odds on that happening? Chris traded with me so I have a gift to remember. We sat on Santa's knee (only the ladies of course) as we told him whether we had been good or bad. Much fun!!! It was a real festive Christmas Eve as we retired to the bar. My concern that I would miss Christmas at home was forgotten as this wonderful crew made it a festive fun night. Again, I must add here that this was a wonderful group of leaders not only informative but fun.

CHAPTER 27

SNARES ISLAND

Day 23 Thursday, December 25, 2003, Christmas Day

Latitude/Longitude:	48°29'S, 166°38'E
Wind:	S, 14 knots
Air Temperature:	10°C/50°F
Sea Temperature:	11°C/52°F

Ole Saint Nick gave us a Christmas gift today and that was calmer seas. We even had the best sleep in three nights. Now that was a real gift.

At breakfast time we approached Ho Ho Bay (yes that is what it says on the Admiralty charts) in the Snares. Now I call that real planning. Unfortunately there was a big swell. The Captain tried several different positions and anchorages, but in each case the rise and fall by the gangway made it unsafe to disembarkation into the zodiacs. It is a very difficult operation and for that reason the planned zodiac landing was aborted.

The birders were happy as there were many birds flying about the ship. There were Sooty Shearwaters, a number of Buller's and Salvin's Albatrosses soaring past, plus the odd Royal Albatross delighting everyone. We always had the petrels diving below us in the clear water. I did not see the Snares Crested Penguins that came to inspect the ship but they were small in numbers and shy. I did not spend much time on the deck because of the cold wind so I do not have much to write about the birds of the area. Many of the birders spent hours on the deck oblivious of the wind. My interest was in seeing and filming the penguins.

I must say that the Captain did try every possibility to take us ashore in Zodiacs. He looked for sheltered coves that might avoid the heavy swell. But to no avail the raise and fall of the gangway platform just made it impossible to accomplish. The real danger was the ship's roll. There were regularly over nine feet swells resulting that there was a real danger of getting the Zodiac fouled under the fenders.

However, one Zodiac was launched because we had to pick up a shore party of four New Zealanders that had been monitoring Sooty Shearwater numbers off the Snares. Two loads of equipment and rucksacks were brought out from their summer camp and hoisted onto the foredeck. They were able to unload this equipment without any problem with the Zodiacs operations however, when it was time to bring the four researchers aboard it was dangerous. The transferring them from the Zodiac to the platform was dangerous because they could not secure the Zodiac to the platform in the conventional way. They had to choose their moment and leap.

All went well, but there was never any question of our Zodiac cruising, to everyone's disappointment including Susan, the Captain, and crew. Needless to say, there were many unhappy passengers. It was a beautiful day, with perfect light for photography and a great view of some highly picturesque islands.

We had a fascinating briefing session when Corey Bragg the New Zealand head and station commander spoke to us in his native tongue of Maori. Then he spoke perfect English. These young people who do research are so well educated and devoted to preserving this earth and environment.

He told us of their everyday existence on Snares. I have such an admiration for these young people who have to live in such dire conditions. It was quite a contrast to their life on the island and the luxury of the ship.

Now this is Christmas Day. Olaf, our chef prepared us an American Christmas Dinner, followed by more carol singing and visits to Elke in the bar. It was my second memorable Christmas Day.

Now are you ready for this—the 26th was Boxing Day, our Russian Christmas celebration. We had the Captain's Farewell Cocktail Party and a wonderful Russian dinner. There were little shot glasses with Russian vodka. We toasted with straight shots of vodka and Beluga caviar. Of course we had borsch, fish course and meatballs and Russian wines throughout the dinner.

Do remember this is expedition cruising at its best. I love cruising and the wonderful meals. We were entertained after this wonderful dinner by all the Russians in their native costumes, this talent and costumes were a requirement for working on the ship.

Here Is A Picture of Me with the Waitresses

This day was an easy passage from Snares with only the gentlest of rolling. We had a lecture to prepare us for departure and settling of bar and radio bills. We then packed to go home.

CHAPTER 28

Today is the day we depart. I have made new friends and had a great adventure. The most memorable days were with the penguins. It was a special gift from the "Weather Gods" to have that beautiful light that day at Cape Washington. Then there was the group of males on Coulman Island that tobogganed in and stopped right in front of me so I could photograph them up close. They are known to be curious and they probably wanted to see what that red and yellow thing with a tripod and camera was doing.

As the crew waved us off we boarded a bus at the port at Lyttleton, New Zealand. It was a hot summer day. This was such a contrast to the wintry weather that we were in for all those days at sea.

Driving through Lyttleton I enjoyed what a quaint country it is with it is beautiful English gardens. Everything was so fresh and clean.

A bus took us to Christchurch where we had time to visit the Antarctica museum. It was a wonderful exhibit of the penguins.

We flew from there to Auckland to make the flight home. When I arrived at the Quantas Airport was the time I really felt unhappy about being alone. It was very hot and I was dressed for the summer but unfortunately wore a traveling black polyester pant outfit and it was too hot. Now we had to go from the Domestic Airport to the International Airport to board my flight to LAX. Now there was a van without a driver that was supposed to drive the mile to the International departure. I decided that I was running short of time so started walking. I don't know what happened to my fellow cruisers but I was alone. Now I had to carry my entire luggage. Yes, the luggage had wheels but it was the weight of the combination of equipment and clothes. I just made it to the departure gate when I went to check in the weight of my carry-on luggage which was my camera and laptop were 3 pounds over weight and they would not let me board. I had to go back to the check-in desk and they refused to let me take my camera and laptop in the roll-along case. I have traveled too much to send my equipment through with the luggage. My husband had photo equipment stolen in Buenos Aires. Now remember I am running out of time for my flight and I am trying to work out this problem.

Well, they sent me to the supervisor and she was just mean because when I ask if the flight was full and it was not full so weight was not a problem. She insisted that it was because I was flying coach. The airline would not grant the business class seat that I had the frequent flyer mileage for because I had planned the flight just a month before flying and they said there were no seats available. There were plenty of empty seats in business and first class.

I have traveled the world and this was the worst treatment I have ever experienced and I wonder to this day if my good-looking husband had been alive to argue the case it would not have been a problem.

I truly suffered physically from having to carry my camera pack and my laptop in the plastic bag they gave me. My arms ached for days afterwards. This flight was doomed. Again I had a beautiful 4-year-old boy as a row companion and when he finally was sleepy he stretched out on the floor. His head was beneath my feet. His father said that is where he slept when he was that age. Honestly, I do love 4-year-old boys. Between my hassles to board, my exhaustion from carrying all the weight I literally slept and never left my seat for 12 hours. Flying is requirement not a pleasure.

The reason I am writing this is because when you are alone you have no one to commiserate with or to help you. One of my bridge buddies stood guard over my cart at the baggage claim. I miss the days when we had red caps that you could pay to help with the luggage.

When all is written my memories of that beautiful experience I had cruising through Antarctica is what I will always remember. I saved some great shots of the penguins and I am hoping my movie will make people who view it love the penguins and scenery as much as I do. There is still a lot of beauty on this earth. I will never let cold temperatures and rough seas stop me from enriching my life.

We all should be concerned about the icebergs and glaciers melting and the rising of the sea temperatures and if I can make one person aware of this phenomena I will do so by writing. The fairy penguins in Tasmania are starving because the warmer water has killed off the fish. The B15A that has been in the news is the iceberg that I had the ice from in my drink. It is responsible for a whole generation of chicks not surviving. I spoke with Quark and the B15A was moving south about a mile a day. We will not know until next season how many of the chicks survived.

Here in Southern California where I live the rains we are having could be a result of this melting. The glaciers in Switzerland are also melting and moving.

When traveling I am always aware of the distances I have to travel to these expedition destinations and yet feel the earth is so small. I have found beauty, serenity, people, animals, ships and crews that make me so thankful to be alive and enjoying the experience.

Life can be so beautiful if we just take the time to adventure into the world of nature. I hope you have enjoyed my adventure.

GLORIA IN CABIN ON KAPITAN KHLEBNEKOV

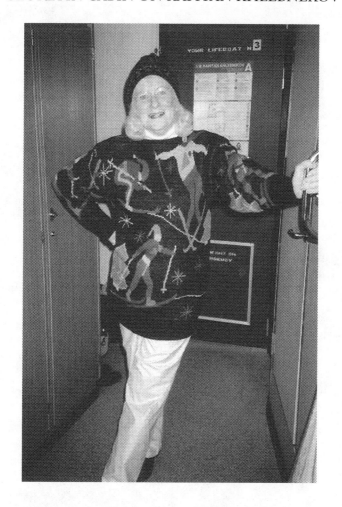

The film (coupon is at the back of the book) I took on Cape Washington and Coulman Island I am including with the journal so that you not only read but can experience the wonderful scenes I took. The film is not long and you can take a break from reading and watch some of the film so that you feel like you are there.

My favorite shots are of "my boys" the group of male Emperor Penguins that came right up to me so I could photograph them and then returned to the sea. That was a gift to me.

TUXEDO JUNCTION
THE LORDS OF ANTARCTICA
DVD

To really enjoy my adventure of Antarctica
and the Emperor penguins this film will
take you there. The scenes are fantastic.
The colors are beautiful.

You can get the DVD for $9.99

Plus Shipping

Credit Cards Accepted
American Express / Master Card or Visa
Card Number _____

Mail this coupon to:

G.L. Clifford
1650 Park Newport Apt#217
Newport Beach, CA 92660

Or

E-mail me at:
gloriaclifford@att.net

Name _____
Address _____
        _____
        _____
Telephone _____
e-mail _____
        _____